20

Legal

Pitfalls

for

Nurses

to

Avoid

Delmar Publishers' Online Services

To access Delmar on the World Wide Web, point your browser to:

http://www.delmar.com/delmar.html

To access through Gopher: gopher://gopher.delmar.com

(Delmar Online is part of "thomson.com", an Internet site with information on
more than 30 publishers of the International Thomson Publishing organization.)

For information on our products and services:

email: info@delmar.com

or call 800-347-7707

20 Legal Pitfalls for Nurses to Avoid

Janine Fiesta, BSN, JD
Lehigh Valley Hospital
Department of Legal Services
Allentown, Pennsylvania

Delmar Publishers Inc.™

I T P™

NOTICE TO THE READER

Cover Design: J^2 Designs

Delmar Publishing Team
Publisher: David C. Gordon
Senior Acquisitions Editor: Bill Burgower
Assistant Editor: Debra M. Flis
Project Editor: Danya M. Plotsky
Production Coordinator: Barbara A. Bullock
Art and Design Coordinators: Megan K. DeSantis
                                Timothy J. Conners

For information, address

Delmar Publishers Inc.
3 Columbia Circle, Box 15015,
Albany, NY 12212-5015

COPYRIGHT © 1994 BY DELMAR PUBLISHERS INC.

The trademark ITP is used under license.

Printed in the United States of America
Published simultaneously in Canada
by Nelson Canada,
a division of The Thomson Corporation

    3 4 5 6 7 8 9 10 XXX 00 99 98 97 96

Library of Congress Cataloging-in-Publication Data

Fiesta, Janine.
    20 legal pitfalls for nurses to avoid / Janine Fiesta.
        p. cm — (Real nursing series)
    Includes index.
    ISBN 0-8273-6152-1
    1 Nurses—Malpractice—United States. 2. Nursing—Law and legislation—United States.
I. Title. II. Title: Twenty legal pitfalls for nurses to avoid. III. Series.
KF2915.N83F52   1994
346.7303'32—dc20   93-34184
[347.306332]   CIP

REALNURSING SERIES
Alice M. Stein, MA, RN, Series Editor
Medical College of Pennsylvania

HEALING YOURSELF: A NURSE'S GUIDE TO SELF-CARE AND RENEWAL
COMMUNICATION AND IMAGE IN NURSING
FEAR AND AIDS/HIV: EMPATHY AND COMMUNICATION
SEXUAL HEALTH: A NURSE'S GUIDE
20 LEGAL PITFALLS FOR NURSES TO AVOID
TO LISTEN, TO COMFORT, TO CARE: REFLECTIONS ON DEATH AND DYING
THE NURSE AS HEALER
MEDICATION ERRORS: THE NURSING EXPERIENCE

FUTURE TITLES:
CRITICAL BUSINESS SKILLS FOR NURSES
HEALING ALCOHOL AND SUBSTANCE ABUSE
ETHICAL DILEMMAS IN NURSING
WAR STORIES: DIFFICULT NURSING DECISIONS
THE FEMINIST NURSE
THE GAY AND LESBIAN NURSE
INTERVENTIONS IN EVERYDAY NURSING EMERGENCIES
HEALING RACISM IN NURSING

able of Contents

Preface

In order for the nurse to minimize liability exposure, there are numerous common pitfalls (or bear traps!) that should be avoided. While it is true that anyone can sue anyone for anything, it is also true that many liability situations can be minimized through reasonable nursing practices or even in some cases, avoided, as in the informed consent example.

The list of common pitfalls presented in this book represent the most frequently encountered liability areas. Included in each chapter are risk management tips to maximize defensibility and the avoidance of claims. Both an informal format and the inclusion of humor are a deliberate attempt to aid the reader in learning and reading with enjoyment. As with any legal text, the advice given is not meant to apply to specific situations but is general guidance and a reflection of current legal cases and concepts. Because case law changes daily and may differ from jurisdiction to jurisdiction, the reader should consult risk management/legal counsel for specific advice.

To assist the reader in understanding this book, the following definitions should be kept in mind.

Pitfall: also known as a *bear trap*

Pit: any nursing unit

Fall: action taken by a patient that a nurse may have just left five minutes ago who was alert, oriented and told to stay in bed and/or the patient who was appropriately and securely restrained.

Bear: more commonly called doctor; may be mean, nasty, arrogant, controlling or pleasant, cheerful, cuddly (as in teddy bear) - this may be the same physician during the same day.

Trap: what nurses frequently walk into when management says "you must float" and the nurse says "no". Or when the doctor says, "Do not wake me up at night under any circumstances: and the nurse says "yes", or when the patient says "I never took a yellow pill before" and the nurse does not listen.

Chapter 1

Neglecting to Make Safety a High Priority

Hippocrates' command to "do no harm" is a recognition that the provision of medical care can, in fact, be dangerous. Despite everyone's efforts, patients do become injured while in the hospital. The phrase used to describe such injury is iatrogenic injury, and studies suggest that the possibility of such occurrences is very high.[1] The Tort system, which allows financial compensation for acts of negligence that cause harm or injury, is often criticized for failing to compensate all the legitimate claims and yet sometimes compensating financially for non-legitimate claims.

In fact, a common suggestion to correct the problems in the current Tort system has been to implement a no-fault insurance system for malpractice cases, which would function like the workers' compensation system in that certain injuries would be automatically compensated regardless of their cause. This would eliminate the need to have a jury determine who was at fault. Unfortunately, the studies evaluating this idea suggest that it is not an economically feasible alternative. Using New York statistics, a Harvard Medical Practice Study found that 1 out of 8 incidents of malpractice currently results in the filing of a claim.[2] In an earlier California study, only 1 out of 10 incidents of malpractice resulted in the filing of a claim.[3] Under a no-fault system, the number of required compensations would be much greater.

It seems, then, that malpractice suits are here to stay, and all personnel can be affected. Since all individuals are responsible for their own acts of negligence, both professional and nonprofessional health care providers have been held legally accountable **(liable)** for their actions and omissions.[4] For this reason, meeting the safety needs of patients needs to be a high-priority issue for the employer, who may be exposed to **corporate liability** from failure to orient employees to this most basic of patient care principles. As with most malpractice cases, it is often the less complex aspects of patient care that result in liability and injury. Ignoring basics is always dangerous.

FALLS: A COMMON INJURY

Some of the most common injuries are falls. Both professional and nonprofessional health care providers—including nursing assistants, orderlies, and volunteers—have experienced liability because a patient has fallen and received an injury. In fact, the professional nurse is more likely to appear in a courtroom in his or her career lifetime because of such an occurrence than for any other single reason. Falls, then, can be a major legal pitfall, and there are several ways to protect oneself.

Documenting Instructions

Not all falls are preventable: they will happen. However, liability does not occur simply because a patient has fallen and received an injury.[5] It occurs only when the injury is a result of the nurse's failure to follow a reasonable professional standard of care for the patient. If an alert, oriented, competent patient has been told not to get out of bed without assistance and he or she ignores this instruction, a fall with injury should not result in a liability finding against the health care provider. Therefore, one way to prevent the liability pitfall is to document the instructions given to the patient. Health teaching and patient instructions are usually very significant documentation.

Documenting Noncompliance

One defense in malpractice cases is **contributory or comparative negligence**. This defense applies when noncompliant, competent patients contribute to their own injury. In some instances, noncompliant behavior may prevent the patient from receiving any financial compensation. In other situations, the patient may be held only partly liable and so may not be fully compensated.

In one fall case a 62-year-old patient who had a cervical laminectomy experienced left-sided weakness postoperatively. He took a sleeping pill, walked to the bathroom alone, and fell several times. These injuries rendered him a triplegic, and he died from pneumonia 3 years later. The nursing staff was held negligent for failing to raise the side rail and to assist him to the bathroom. However, the patient was found comparatively negligent and the award was reduced by 23%.[6]

To prevent liability, noncompliant patient behavior should always be charted at the time it occurs. Such behavior includes failing to follow instructions, refusing medication, leaving the hospital against medical advice, ignoring dietary instruction, and tampering with equipment at the bedside (many orthopedic nurses will recognize the problem of the recovering young male patient who spends his time in bed rearranging his traction).

Identifying High-Risk Patients

Since falls are often not preventable and every patient has the potential while in the hospital to sustain an injury from a fall, it is important to attempt to identify high-risk patients. These may include patients with impaired vision or balance, patients who are sedated, or patients with a history of falls as well as those who are confused. It is not easy to make this identification. However, elderly patients who have never been hospitalized before should definitely be considered high risk on their first night in the hospital. These patients often awaken during the night to use the bathroom and may become confused and disoriented by the unfamiliar environment. Eliminating total darkness in the room may help. In addition, instructing them to notify the nurse upon awakening may be useful.

The continuing aging of the inpatient population suggests that fall-related claims are likely to increase.[7] Every year, one-third of Americans 65 or older who live at home and two-thirds of those in nursing homes will fall at least once. Between 10% and 25% of these individuals will incur serious injuries from a fall. Use of medication may increase the risk of falling.[8] All these incidents will continue to be costly. In one study, the average payment for the Harvard-affiliated hospitals between 1976 and 1989 was $10,482 for patients who fell.[9] St. Paul's Fire and Marine Insurance Company reports that the average fall-related claim paid for 1989 was $16,580.[10]

Applying Restraints When Necessary

Once a high-risk patient is identified, appropriate intervention may include 24-hour attendance by the family after they have been educated about fall prevention, a private-duty nurse, relocation of the patient near the nursing station, the use of a bed check, more frequent monitoring by nursing staff, or the use of restraints. As a general rule, in the acute care setting, the nurse is more likely to be held liable for failing to restrain a patient who should be restrained than for restraining one who should not be. Restraints can therefore become a major concern.

Failure to apply restraints was the issue in a Pennsylvania decision. The patient jumped from a hospital window and suffered multiple fractures. The family blamed improper steroid prescription and the failure to apply restraints despite signs of steroid psychosis. A nurse had noted that the woman was having delusions and felt that she should be watched closely and that restraints should be considered. When the patient argued with nurses about taking her medication, the physician was called. He came and calmed the patient down but left without ordering restraints. It was soon after this that the obese patient squeezed through a 13-inch window opening. The doctor testified that he did not order restraints because he felt they would only make her more agitated. A verdict for the defendants therefore was returned by the jury and the patient received no compensation.[11]

Since restraints themselves may pose a danger to the patient, it is also important to orient employees to their correct application. Moreover, it is well recognized that some patients are able to get out of restraints in almost Houdini fashion. Use of the bed occupancy monitor may not always prevent a fall from occurring, though it does help provide prompt assistance for the patient who has fallen.

Handling Occurrences with Honesty

Some of the liability for nurses in fall cases has resulted from failure to properly care for the patient after the incident has occurred. It is especially important to notify the patient's physician. In addition the patient's family should always be informed as soon as possible. Even without an apparent injury, the family may suspect some type of cover-up or misrepresentation if they are not told about the event.

In all such cases, honesty is the best policy. Covering up or even forgetting or neglecting to tell the family may result in anger and destroy the relationship with the patient and family. All experienced risk managers know that the number one requirement for a malpractice lawsuit is not malpractice but an unhappy patient, because it takes an angry or upset patient and/or family to visit a lawyer's office. If the result of an injury is unexpected or a complication has occurred, whether a lawsuit follows often depends on the perception of events and the degree of rapport between the health care provider and the patient. Thus the ability to communicate caring and compassion in an honest manner is important in the prevention of malpractice cases.

Avoiding Assumptions

Careful and precise documentation is also important. For example, if the nurse walks into the room and finds the patient lying on the floor next to the bed, the nurse should not chart "patient fell out of bed." This is an assumption about what happened, not what the nurse actually saw, and may expose the nurse to liability unnecessarily.

Assumptions are always dangerous; they are capable of harming both patients and health care providers. Moreover, they are all too easy to make. As an illustration, one night a surgeon received a phone call from one of his male patients. The man, obviously agitated, reported that his wife was having great pain in her abdomen and he feared appendicitis. The doctor paused for a minute and said, "But John, I removed your wife's appendix last year and no one has a second appendix." After a moment's hesitation the man explained that this was his second wife.[12] If the doctor had made his assumption silently and it had gone uncorrected, this situation could have had serious results. You will find other examples of dangerous assumptions in this book as you read.

SAFETY IN THE OVERALL ENVIRONMENT

Failure to maintain a safe environment extends beyond fall cases. In one hospital, for example, the local Girl Scouts prepared favors for patients to place on their Christmas trays. These "favors" were distributed by the volunteers and consisted of a snow scene in a closed container that could be turned over to produce a blizzard effect. On Christmas Day an elderly, confused patient drank his snow scene, thinking that any liquid on his tray was meant to be ingested. The snow crystals were moth flakes and the patient had to have his stomach pumped.

The obligation to ensure a safe environment extends to all hospital departments as well as to the hospital itself under corporate liability principles. As a health care provider, the corporate entity has its own set of legal obligations. One challenge hospitals face is keeping not only patients but also visitors safe. Again, elderly visitors are especially at risk from falls. Ice or snow is an example of a situation where visitor injury may occur even when all prudent care is taken. In one unreported decision, an elderly man fell in the parking lot and lost his eye. He was not following the identified path for walking and tripped over a high curb. In a recent Missouri case, the court found that a hospital had no duty to remove ice and snow from its parking lot because the frozen precipitation was the result of a general weather condition affecting the area, and the visitor was aware of the icy condition of the lot before she fell.[13]

Risk management steps can be taken to help minimize liability in such instances. For example, employees who see a visitor fall should direct the visitor to the emergency department for a medical evaluation. Most hospitals will pick up the cost of such a visit, recognizing that if the visitor returns the following day with a serious injury, it cannot always be determined that the injury was incurred after the individual fell at the hospital. The risk manager should also be immediately notified so that a photograph of the location of the incident can be taken. This is especially important when the visitor is alleging a serious injury caused by an obstacle or allegedly dangerous condition either caused by the hospital or allowed to exist because the hospital failed to prevent it or take care of it. All personnel—including nurses—should be aware of these risks and cooperate in preventing liability.

NOTES

1. National Association of Insurance Commissioners. (1980) NAIC, closed claims. In *Malpractice claims: Medical malpractice closed claims, 1975–1978* (p. 303). NAIC; U.S. General Accounting Office. (1987, April). Characteristics of claims closed. In *Medical malpractice: Characteristics of claims closed in 1984* (p. 24).

2. (1990). Patients, doctors and lawyers: Medical injury, malpractice litigation and patient compensation in New York. Cambridge: Harvard University Press.

3. Danzon, Patricia M. (1985) *Medical malpractice: Theory, evidence and public policy*. Cambridge: Harvard University Press.

4. Fiesta, Janine. (1988). *The law and liability: A guide for nurses* (2nd ed., p. 24). New York: Wiley.

5. Fiesta, Janine. (1985). Nursing Liability-The Patient Who Falls. *Orthopedic Nursing, 4* (3), 59–61.

6. Donaldson v. Harper Grace Hospital, Wayne County, No. 88-808854.

7. Brown, Cheli. (1991) Identifying High Risk Patients is Key to Reducing Patient Falls, *Hospital Risk Management. 13* (12), 149–152.

8. Studies Identify Which Elderly are Most Likely to Suffer from Falls. *The Morning Call*, Allentown, PA (1989, August).

9. Tan, M.W. (1991). Risk management foundation for the Harvard medical institutions. Forum, 12, (1) 11.

10. Update. (1990). The *St. Paul's 1990 annual report to policyholders*. Minnesota.

11. Melley v. Penater, M.D. and Gnaden Huetten Hospital, No. 90-555 (Pa 1991).

12. Engelberg, Adele. (1992) In The Jocular Vein. *Medical Economics*, 184.

13. Willis V. Springhill Memorial Hospital, 804 S.W. 2d 416 (Mo. Ap. 1991).

Chapter 2

Failing to Spot and Report Possible Violence

Failure to protect against criminal activity and violence is also a pitfall for the hospital. More and more frequently cases are appearing that deal with crimes occurring within the hospital environment. To protect the hospital against liability, nurses should report any suspicions they have of criminal activity at once.

INTRUDERS AND KIDNAPPERS

The hospital's corporate liability includes accountability for security. The violent death of a pathologist at a New York hospital highlighted the many problems hospitals face. Among those security-related charges that have been leveled against hospitals are improperly training security personnel, failing to have appropriate security policies in place, failing to follow policies, neglecting background checks, and retaining a known criminal employee. In the New York case, the hospital hired more police guards after the former mental patient, clothed in blue hospital gown, was charged with raping and murdering the pathologist.

In another case, a maternity patient was brutally assaulted in the middle of the night in her room on the second floor of the hospital. The male trespasser had been noticed earlier on the fourth floor by a visitor who was trying to sleep in the visitors' lounge. The visitor reported the man's strange behavior to the nursing staff, who called hospital security personnel. Before the security guard arrived, however, the crime was committed. The assailant was no stranger to the hospital. According to the security reports, he had been seen at the hospital three times prior to the incident, had been suspected of stealing, and had been arrested once for trespassing. At trial, the security director testified that the 381-bed hospital had three night security officers. After evening visiting hours, two guards were stationed outside while the third guard covered the floors. The appeals court found that the hospital had been warned of the trespasser's presence and dangerous nature.[1] In this case, then, the hospital was held liable because the crime was foreseeable.

If the potential for harm is not foreseeable, however, hindsight should not be used to impose liability. In *Hendley v. Springhill Memorial Hospital*,[2] a hospital and a provider of physical therapy services were not held liable for an unauthorized vaginal examination performed on a patient by a pain control device vendor. The patient was admitted for pain in her coccyx, and her physician prescribed a Tens unit. The Tens vendor went to the patient's room to check on the unit and found it was not functioning properly. The patient testified that while the vendor was fixing the unit he asked her if she had pain during sex. When she responded she sometimes did, he performed a vaginal examination, during which he questioned her about points of tenderness. Later in the day the patient, who had become suspicious about what had happened, asked hospital personnel about the appropriateness of the exam. When she heard that such treatment was unauthorized, she officially notified the hospital about the alleged incident and also told her husband, who called the police. The court held that the hospital should not be held responsible.[3]

Kidnappings in newborn nurseries are also a security problem. For example, a nurse enters a hospital room and tells a new mother that she must take the baby to be tested or weighed. The mother does not know that the nurse is an imposter and that an abduction has just occurred. Fortunately, in the majority of kidnapping cases the infant eventually is recovered and returned unharmed to the parents. Unfortunately, however, the number of kidnapping occurrences has increased in recent years.

At the 659-bed Jackson-Madison County General Hospital in Jackson, Tennessee, an infant was handed by her mother to two women who said they had to take the baby's footprints. Contrary to previously published reports, the women were wearing street clothes and not hospital uniforms. The mother, however, believed that they were employees because "other people who worked in the hospital did not wear uniforms." The child was found 12 hours later outside a nearby hospital. The parents filed a lawsuit claiming the hospital took too long (allegedly over 2 hours) to discover that the child was missing.

In 1983, a 12-hour-old infant boy was taken from a nursery crib at the 500-bed University of Mississippi Medical Center in Jackson, Mississippi. Nurses allegedly thought the abductor, a woman, was its mother. At the 834-bed Parkland Memorial Hospital in Dallas, Texas, a woman posing as a nurse took a 3-day-old from its mother. At the 768-bed University Hospital in Augusta, Georgia, a few months later, a mother handed her 3-day-old to a woman posing as a nurse.[4]

In November 1986, a newborn boy was taken from his mother's arms by a woman dressed in a lab coat who said she was taking the child for an examination. The incident occurred in a Pennsylvania hospital. The mother's pastor, who was visiting with her at the time, reportedly became suspicious almost immediately when he heard a door close across the hall. From that time until a week later when the baby was found unharmed by the FBI, the story was featured nationally by all the media. The distraught parents appeared on television pleading for the return of their newborn son. Friends of the couple offered a $27,000 reward. A sketch of the alleged kidnapper was shown and distributed, and the baby was found in the company of a 44-year-old woman and her 42-year-old boyfriend. The couple was indicted for the crime, and the woman reportedly told the FBI that she had had a hysterectomy several years previously and wanted to "steal a baby for herself by dressing up as a nurse and going into the hospital."[5]

A preventive program to anticipate infant kidnapping is vital. A specific obstetrical security plan should be developed by the security department with the assistance of nursing and risk management. As part of this plan, careful attention should be given to identification. Identification badges with photographs should be worn by everyone. Visitor policies to the obstetrical area should be strictly enforced, and the hospital may also wish to consider badges for visitors. Access to the nursery and from the building should be secured. Finally, mothers should be informed of the need for vigilance and should have some way of verifying the identity of a nurse before returning their baby.

The hospital's responsibility in all such cases is measured by the vulnerability of the patient and the foreseeability of the danger. Before the first kidnapping case, it was not foreseeable that such an incident would occur in a hospital. Once it did happen, hospitals were put on notice of the possibility and a higher standard of reasonable care was applied.

HOSPITAL PERSONNEL

Nurses and other hospital employees can also commit serious crimes. Although the majority of legal cases involving nurses are classified as civil cases, an increasing number are appearing in the criminal court system. *Deadly Medicine* (subtitled *The True and Chilling Story of a Pediatric Nurse Who Killed for the Thrill*), a best-seller which later appeared as a television movie, focused attention on the criminal activities of one nurse. The trial of a nurse charged with administering high doses of morphine to a terminally ill patient received notoriety in Massachusetts—and it, too, became a television movie.[6] These movies were highly rated: not only are the cases occurring, but the public is becoming aware that health care workers may be engaged in criminal activity.

Although these two incidents have received widespread attention, they are not unique examples of criminal activity in the health care system. In Georgia, a registered nurse was accused of injecting 11 patients with potassium chloride, causing six deaths. An investigation began after nine cardiac arrests occurred in the unit during the first three weeks of the month when usually only three or four arrests occurred per month. The nurse was convicted of aggravated assault with intent to murder. She was found guilty but mentally ill on only one charge.

In another incident, a 35-year-old nurse's aide at Cincinnati's Daniel Drake Memorial Hospital was convicted of murdering 21 patients under his care in a 12-month time period. The killer, Donald Harvey, knew enough about his victims' illnesses to choose a method of death that would not be suspected and usually could not be detected. He confessed to at least 50 murders since the early 1970s.

An interesting issue in these so-called Angel of Death cases involving large numbers of victims is how these situations could occur without other personnel becoming aware that something unusual was happening. In all of these investigations at least one nurse admitted concern and suspicion that something untoward had occurred. Apparently, however, they did not act on their suspicions. It is important to remember that a nurse who suspects that patient injury may be occurring intentionally or negligently has a *legal duty* to report the suspicion to his or her supervisor. An appropriate investigation will determine whether the suspicions are unfounded, and as long as the nurse is acting in good faith and without malice, there should be no concern about repercussions for reporting a concern that turns out to be erroneous.

Health care workers also have been involved in other criminal activities. A Colorado hospital was required to pay $156,000 in damages to a patient who was sexually assaulted by a hospital employee. A 23-year-old woman recovering from a suicide attempt at the hospital was sexually assaulted twice while she was restrained in her bed. Eleven days prior to the attack, the employee had pled guilty of sexually assaulting a patient at another hospital where he had worked. The suit alleged that the hospital negligently failed to protect patients from employees' criminal acts, failed to properly screen employees, failed to discharge a known sexual offender, and failed to provide adequate security.[7]

Charges of infanticide filed against parents and the attending physician of newborn Siamese twins in Danville, Illinois, brought to public attention the possibility of criminal activity in intensive care nurseries—at the request of parents, and by the order of physicians.[8] A nurse faced with such a situation should immediately notify the nurse manager, who should notify administration and risk management or legal counsel immediately. Neither a physician nor the family may authorize a criminal activity, and a high degree of suspicion should be a red flag. In all such cases, nurses should follow their instincts.

RELATIVES

A family member may also criminally abuse a patient in a hospital. In *Coles v. Chester Haworth et al.*[9], a patient suffering from arsenic poisoning was given a final lethal dose while in the hospital. The patient had been transferred from another hospital. Elevated levels of arsenic had been found, but because there was a 9-day delay in notification as a result of the transfer, the dose given by the husband was fatal.

Assessing a particular individual's potential for violence is not easy. When Rudy Linares walked into the pediatric unit of Rush-Presbyterian-St. Luke's with a .357 Magnum and unplugged his son's life support system, there was little that health care providers could do to prevent his actions, nor could they anticipate them. Because 16-month-old Samuel was not brain dead, Mr. Linares had been instructed to obtain a court order to terminate treatment. A murder charge was filed against the father.

Violence against children often takes the form of parental neglect. In virtually all jurisdictions, statutes prohibit, except under emergency circumstances, the medical treatment of minors without the consent of one of their parents. These statutes acknowledge the general beliefs that parents have the prerogative to direct the course of their minor child's medical treatment and that parents will use their judgment in their child's best interests. However, a parent's right to make decisions on their child's behalf is not absolute. Whenever evidence suggests that the parents are derelict in discharging their duties—for example, by failing to provide "necessary" medical care—the courts will intervene.

In *Hall v. State*,[10] a jury found the parents of a child who died of acute bronchial pneumonia guilty of reckless homicide. The evidence presented showed that the child had been ill for some 5 days but that the parents, because of their religious beliefs, had failed to seek medical care for him. The court held that there was no merit to the parents' contention that their exercise of prayer in lieu of medical care brought their reckless conduct within the realm of acceptable standards of conduct.

In another case, the court held a mother subject to criminal prosecution for the death of her 4-year-old daughter. She was charged with **involuntary manslaughter** and **child endangerment.** The appellate court held that the penal code, under which it is a misdemeanor for a parent to fail to furnish a child with such remedial care as food, shelter, and medical treatment, did not insulate a parent against charges of involuntary manslaughter or endangerment when a lack of medical attention resulted in the death of a child. The court pointed out that in California it has long been recognized that the failure to exercise due care in the treatment of another, where a duty to furnish such care exists, constitutes a form of manslaughter resulting from an act of omission. The point at which a parent may incur liability for substituting prayer treatment for medical care is clearly that point at which the lack of medical attention places the child in a situation endangering the child's person or health. The court stated that the exact point at which that occurs, however, can only be determined by a jury.

In all such cases, where the parents' judgment appears to be clearly contrary to the welfare of a child, the health care provider is required to act as an advocate for the child. In the hospital setting, a staff nurse may be the first person who identifies this scenario. That nurse has the duty to communicate this information to the physician and to the nurse manager, who should then seek counsel to determine the appropriate action.

The issue of a mother endangering the life of the child in utero is a challenging dilemma in obstetrics practice. In California, a woman was charged with a criminal misdemeanor for contributing to the death of her baby boy by failing to follow her doctor's advice before the infant's birth. Although suffering from placenta previa, she ignored advice to seek immediate medical assistance if she began to hemorrhage. She was also accused of taking amphetamines and smoking marijuana during her pregnancy.[11] When a home care or outpatient nurse becomes aware of such a situation, she should inform her supervisor.

Intentionally causing harm to another is not limited to obstetrics or pediatrics. In Montana, Michael Mally was convicted for failing to provide medical care for his wife after she was found injured in their home. Before her injury, Kay Mally had already been in poor physical condition. She suffered from chronic hepatitis, biliary cirrhosis, osteoarthritis, and obesity. She also was an alcoholic and had small areas of cystic degeneration in the brain. She had been diagnosed with liver and kidney disease. After she fell, her husband picked her up and placed her in the bedroom, where she remained without medical assistance for two days. When an ambulance was eventually called, she was unconscious.[12]

Unfortunately, some cases involve nurses' alleged attempts to harm their own family members. In Pennsylvania, a nurse was charged with attempted homicide after she injected her 88-year-old mother with potassium. Her mother was a patient at a nursing home and had suffered a stroke.[13] A pediatric nurse in New York was charged with asphyxiating two of her own newborn babies and trying to kill a third.[14] In New Jersey, a nurse law student was convicted of trying to hire a hit man to kill her husband to end their bitter divorce case.[15]

Criminal cases have also been brought against family members for withdrawing life support, but they have been unsuccessful. Recent cases have held a family member who was acting as guardian for a terminally ill patient immune from criminal liability for directing the withdrawal of life-supporting care.[16]

PSYCHIATRIC PATIENTS

Suicidal Patients

Some of the most difficult judgments made by health care professionals are those dealing with the psychiatric patient who may be suicidal. If someone wants to commit suicide badly enough, he or she will find a way to do it. As with infant kidnapping, the legal issue in these cases is whether the patient's actions were foreseeable, and if foreseeable, whether they were preventable. This is really a two-step analysis.

It is interesting to observe, and an obvious pitfall for nurses, that the number of suicide litigations on behalf of psychiatric patients in community hospitals exceeds those of psychiatric institutions. This may reflect a more consistent approach to protecting patients from themselves and others in an environment where this is a constant problem. To prevent liability exposure, the nurse in a nonpsychiatric hospital may have to be especially alert to such problems.

It also would appear, at least anecdotally, that the suicide is more likely to be successful (and therefore a more likely basis for litigation) if the patient is placed in a nonpsychiatric unit in the community hospital, where staff are less frequently involved in the care of these patients.

Once the patient has been identified as a risk for suicide, either through suicidal expressions or actions, and suicide precautions are initiated, follow-through seems to be more consistent if the patient has been placed in a psychiatric unit. As with any issue involving patient care, repetition seems essential in preventing error. (This supports the development of common systems both for patient care and for charting, as discussed in Chapters 6 and 19.)

In a Massachusetts healthcare facility, the patient, age 39, had a 12-year history of depression. He had been a patient of the psychiatrist for 1 year. One month before his death, the decedent was hospitalized for a suicide attempt. During this hospitalization, the psychiatrist ordered 4-minute observations. After 3 weeks of hospitalization, the patient was discharged. Nine days later he was again hospitalized for despondency with suicidal thoughts. The admitting diagnosis was major depression, but no frequent observations were ordered. The patient hung himself in his room with a bed sheet 4 days after admission. The case settled at mediation for $300,000.[17] (One alternative to the trial system is the use of mediation or arbitration. These vehicles provide an alternative to the use of a jury.)

With the suicide issue, as with any clinical issue, *it is important to listen to patients and families carefully.* In a New Jersey case, a man suffering from alcohol withdrawal during hospitalization for a gastrointestinal disorder jumped from a window to his death. The family claimed that the nurse on duty was unaware of precautions for alcohol withdrawal. Moreover, when family members reported that the man was nervous and agitated, the nurse allegedly promised to check on him but never did. A verdict of $1.3 million was returned from the jury.[18]

In another case, a woman who contracted systemic lupus while doing missionary work in Haiti underwent surgery at Cook County Hospital and was given prednisone, which has a recognized side-effect of psychosis. Later she overdosed by taking 50 tablets and had to have her stomach pumped. An intern testified that he then wrote an order for suicide precautions, but the hospital chart revealed no such orders. The patient was placed in a unit that allowed unrestricted access to an unguarded fire escape balcony, from which she jumped to her death. The family contended that the hospital failed to evaluate and treat the decedent for continued suicide risk, and failed to follow and enforce its own protocol for care of patients at increased risk for suicide. The appeals court ruled that the $1.5 million verdict was not excessive.[19]

In this case, the patient's attorney commented in closing argument upon the hospital's failure to produce the only nurse from the psychiatric team who had allegedly evaluated the patient prior to her suicide. He also noted the hospital's failure to produce hospital records ordering and then lifting suicide precautions. The physician testified that he ordered suicide precautions for the patient, but his orders were missing from the hospital records. There was no explanation given as to the whereabouts of those suicide precautions, and the hospital did not call any nurse to testify that he or she had, in fact, provided the one-to-one monitoring required by the order. The plaintiff's counsel implied that the nurse was not produced because her testimony would not have supported the claim that a conscious decision was made to eliminate suicide precautions.

The absence of this nurse illustrates several problems with witnesses. Sometimes a key witness is simply unavailable for trial. Sometimes, too, the witness is not produced purposely because of his or her demeanor, attitude, or personality, since a defensible malpractice case can be lost if a witness is rude, hostile, arrogant, angry, or has an "attitude." If counsel is unable to correct this problem, one alternative sometimes is simply to not use the witness. Of course, if the witness happens to be the defendant in the case, that is not a possible option.

Violent Patients

Failure to prevent a psychiatric patient's violence toward others is also a pitfall. In some cases, the defense can use the theory of **contributory negligence** or **comparative negligence.** In *Freeman v. The Upjohn Co.,*[20] for example, a former police officer blamed the drug Halcion for personality changes that caused him to shoot another man and be given a life sentence in prison. The jury returned a $2.15 million verdict, finding the plaintiff 50% responsible for his crime, the internist 30% negligent, and the manufacturer 20% negligent. The manufacturer was accused of failure to provide adequate warnings. Only the plaintiff's family members were entitled to any award.

The duty of the defendant in psychiatric cases is to follow the same standard as in any malpractice case, one of reasonable care. For example, the treatment team at a psychiatric hospital was not held liable for a male patient's rape of a female patient who had been left alone for approximately 10 minutes after an approved treatment plan. The court found that the hospital had not breached its duty of reasonable care by not continually supervising the male patient or by allowing him to walk unsupervised through the ward during the 10-minute period when the female patient was not under continuous one-to-one supervision, even though the hospital knew of the male patient's sexual interests. In other words, mere sexual interest alone did not make it *foreseeable* that the rape would occur.[21]

The duty to warn a third party of possible harm has also arisen as a cause of liability for the psychiatric clinician. The landmark precedent for this theory is the Tarasoff case, in which a university psychiatrist was held liable for failing to warn a murder victim that specific threats had been made against her life by one of his patients. The patient carried out the threat. The court held that once a physician reasonably determines that a patient poses a serious danger of violence to others, the physician must take action to protect the foreseeable victim of that danger.[22] In many of these cases, because the standard is one of communication of a *specific* threat of violence against some *readily identifiable victim,* any scenario falling short of this does not usually require notification by the physician. For example, in *Wofford v. Eastern State Hospital,*[23] a negligent release action against a hospital was dismissed as too remote and unforeseeable. In this case, the plaintiff's son was released almost 2½ years before he fatally shot his stepfather. No evidence was presented to show that the hospital should have had any indication of the violent propensities of the son.

If there is a specific threat, the duty to inform generally overrides the duty to preserve confidentiality. In *Oringer v. Rotkin,*[24] psychologists informed the police, the victim's family, and the patient's wife of the patient's threats and dangerous nature. This action was proper, since the patient's records indicated that during therapy he had threatened to kill a third party; the psychologist concluded that the patient presented a serious and imminent danger. The court held that there was no breach of confidentiality.

This case illustrates, once again, the importance of judgment. Since the disclosure of confidential information is also a pitfall, the duty to warn must always be balanced against the duty not to disclose. It is always wise to err on the side of safety. Health care providers may complain that these are "catch-22" situations, but the law maintains that they are not. The law is only asking the health care provider to balance the right of confidentiality against the need to know on the basis of careful analysis and the exercise of professional judgment. That is what nurses are taught to do and what they are paid to do.

TRUSTING ONE'S JUDGMENT

All the cases discussed so far concern actual serious crimes and violent behaviors. Of course, it sometimes happens that health care providers presume criminal activity when in fact a crime has not been committed. In *Byers v. City of Reno*,[25] Iola Byers was hospitalized and suffered from a degenerative disease which rendered her dependent upon a respirator. She was placed in the cardiac intensive care unit, and her husband stayed with her. The staff began to notice adjustments on the respirator. Since the respiratory technicians believed they were the only ones in the hospital with the authority to alter respirator settings, they suspected foul play and focused on the husband. He denied their charges. Hospital counsel was notified, who notified the district attorney. Two police officers interviewed and arrested the husband. At the deposition, nurses and doctors testified that they also had the authority to change ventilator settings. The charges against the husband were therefore dropped and he sued the police and the city.

The real mystery in this case was why so many personnel felt that they had authority to adjust something as vital as a respirator without recording changes in the chart or notifying anyone. Thus, as the next chapter will show, the worst crime may have been the lack of policy or the failure to follow policy.[26] Nevertheless, the staff members who suspected criminal activity were right to act on their suspicions, since it is always best to err in favor of patient safety and well-being. Again, when in doubt, *trust your judgment.*

NOTES

1. Roettger v. United Hospitals of St. Paul, Inc., 380 N.W. 2d 856 (Minn. App. 1986).

2. Hendley v. Springhill Memorial Hospital, 575 So. 2d 547 (Ala. 1990).

3. The Citation, August, 1991.

4. Fiesta, Janine. (May, 1990) Security-Whose Liability Infant Kidnapping. *Nursing Management*, p.16..

5. Williams, David A. (1989, Summer). A hospital kidnapping: A risk manager's perspective. *Perspectives in Healthcare Risk Management*, 4, 6.

6. Commonwealth v. Capute, Bristol County Super. Ct., No. 6828 (Mass. October 22, 1981).

7. Callison v. St. Anthony Hospital Systems, No. 86CV10753, Denver District Ct., (July 31, 1987).

8. Horan, Dennis (1982). Infanticide: When doctors orders record murder. *RN Magazine*, 75.

9. Coles v. Chester Haworth et al., (1991). No. 89-CVS-4874. (1991). *Medical Malpractice Verdicts, Settlements & Experts, 4* (11).

10. Hall v. State, 493 N.E. 2d 433 (Ind. 1986).

11. (Jan. 1987), *Journal of the American Bar Association, 3*, 23.

12. State v. Mally. 366 P.2d 868 (Montana, 1961).

13. Title unavailable, Allentown Morning Call, (Sept. 28, 1984).

14. Title unavailable, Allentown Morning Call, (March 4, 1986).

15. 195 Cal. Rptr. 484, (Cal. App. 1983).

16. Title unavailable, Allentown Morning Call, (May 18, 1988).

17. Anonymous v. Anonymous Psychiatrist, No. 663. *Medical Malpractice Verdicts, Settlements & Experts.*

18. Martinez v. St. Elizabeth Hospital. (1993) *Medical Malpractice Verdicts, Settlements & Experts. 9* (2), 25.

19. Eaglin v. Cook County Hospital and Cook County Board of Commissioners, 592 N.E.2d 205 (Ill. 1992).

20. Freeman v. The Upjohn Co. (1993) *Medical Malpractice Verdicts, Settlements & Experts. 9* (2), 16.

21. Millhoff v. Ohio Dept. of Mental Health, 594 N.E.2d 170 (Ohio 1991).

22. Tarasoff v. Regents of the University of California, 551 P.2d 334 (Calif. 1976).

23. Wofford v. Eastern State Hospital, 795 P. 2d 516 (Okla. 1990) .

24. Oringer v. Rotkin, 556 N.Y.S.2d 67 (1990) .

25. Byers v. City of Reno, 663 F. Supp. 94 (Nev. 1987).

26. Action Kit, Horty-Springer. (1988, April). *Patient Care Law.*

Not Following Policies and Standards of Care

Hospitals need policies and standards of care to ensure consistency in patient care and to orient and educate new employees. Very often, not having a policy or having one but not following it can have legal consequences.

INTERNAL STANDARDS

Nursing policies and standards are established in a variety of ways. Internal standards include the nurse's job description as well as the policies and procedures of the institution. Since courts review these references to evaluate what standards of performance are required, the hospital's own internal policy is often a crucial factor in how a case is decided. Hospital rules are also admissible as evidence of standards of care in the community. Whether a hospital or nursing policy establishes a standard of care has been an issue in professional negligence cases.

Nursing manuals, which are routinely used as administrative and educational tools, also define standards of care. For this reason, nurse managers should word them carefully. Staff nurses should review these documents, understand what they are being asked to do and query written requirements that are impossible to follow or establish unrealistic expectations. For example, policies and procedures should be clearly differentiated. In addition, it should be remembered that a policy is a statement of purpose; as such, it usually defines the *minimum* standard for the institution. Words such as *maximum* or *the best* should therefore be used cautiously. Since a minimum standard of care is being defined, this wording subjects personnel to the charge of not acting in accordance with high standards. In other words, the standard should not place an unduly great legal burden on personnel by requiring optimum behavior in every situation. Only reasonable professional standards should be applied.[1]

This warning is important because, as already stated, hospital policies may be used in court. In *Schneider v. Kings Highway Hospital Center*,[2] a clearly written policy existed: hospital regulations stated that bed rails were to be in the upright position for all patients over the age of 70. The patient was found on the floor next to the bed, and the bed rail was down. The patient said that she knew how to lower the rail and had done it herself, but the appeals court said it was more likely that a hospital staff person had lowered it because the patient was weak and elderly. The court ruled against the hospital.

A policy does not have to be in writing to be considered a policy. However, "unwritten" policies increase liability exposure because not all employees may be aware of them. In *Hartman v. Riverside Methodist Hospital*,[3] Regina Hartman came to the hospital for emergency surgery with a full stomach. Fentanyl was administered during surgery. Anesthesia told the recovery room nurse that the patient had a "full stomach," meaning that precautions needed to be taken to prevent aspiration. The nurse administered pain medication, and the patient died of aspiration. This doctor's "unwritten" policy was for nurses not to give drugs without his approval, but his other partners did allow drugs to be administered without specific approval.

One of the most important internal policies is the chain-of-command policy. In the following case, because of a nurse's failure to abide by such a policy, the court found the hospital employer liable to the injured patient. The nursing manual stated that a nurse with any doubt or question about care provided to any patient should direct the question to the attending physician. If the question was not resolved, she or he was to call the department chairperson. In this incident, the patient had a cast, and his arm had become progressively swollen, black, and edematous and was emitting a foul-smelling drainage. He had a high temperature and was at times delirious. The charge nurse called the physician and told him that the patient would not retain oral antibiotics and also reported some other obvious symptoms. She stated at the trial that she also reported the delirium. However, the doctor took no action and the nurse did not call the chairperson. The physician testified that although the nurse did notify him that the patient's condition had worsened, he did not recall her reporting either the foul-smelling drainage or the delirium. He stated that if he had known about these conditions, he would have taken action immediately. The patient's arm was amputated at the shoulder. The court, in giving its opinion, enunciated a classic statement about nurses:

In the dim hours of night, as well as in the light of day, nurses are frequently charged with the duty to observe the condition of the ill and infirm in their care. If that patient, helpless and wholly dependent, shows signs of worsening, the nurse is charged with the obligation of taking some positive action. Every hospital should have a chain-of-command policy to assist the nurse who has a question regarding any aspect of patient care.[4]

EXTERNAL STANDARDS

In judging a case, the court may also use various external standards to determine how a nurse should function. Examples include the Nurse Practice Act of each state, guidelines by the Joint Commission of Accreditation of Healthcare Organizations (JCAHO), and guidelines in textbooks. The Nurse Practice Acts define what the practice of nursing entails in a particular state. Courts look to this legislation for guidance when a case is presented and determine how these laws should be interpreted and applied.

Regularly updated, national, minimum standards may also be used by the courts to establish the minimum standard of care. However, providers should still be allowed to introduce the testimony of experts in their defense. At least one author has suggested that standards should be called "practice parameters" to reduce liability for complying health care providers,[5] since there is almost no standard that can fairly or validly be applied to each and every case. In every nursing malpractice case, in fact, the actions of the nurse defendant are measured against the appropriate nursing standard of care. The issue for the jury is to measure the actions or omissions of the nurse against the performance of a reasonable, prudent nurse with comparable training and experience.

EXTERNAL VERSUS INTERNAL STANDARDS

This means, of course, that sometimes an external standard will override an internal one: whatever is "reasonable" will take precedence. In *Gallagher v. Detroit-Macomb Hospital*,[6] the patient sustained a fractured hip as a result of a fall. He sought to introduce into evidence several nursing policies, including those on using restraints, charting observations, and monitoring changes in behavior. The court excluded the policies, stating that they were merely guidelines for day-to-day activity and did not reflect relevant industry standards or customary usage and practice. The court cited previous holdings of courts in Michigan that the standard of care is established by rules that do not depend on the corporation's own regulations, because these rules may either attempt to lessen the standard owed to the public or impose liability above that which is established by law.[7]

It is important to remember that the standards currently employed in the Tort system are also drawn from *customary practice,* which is established through the testimony of expert witnesses. Originally the standard was the custom prevailing in the particular locality in which the plaintiff received care: this was called the **locality rule**. To prevent local practice from lagging beyond good practice elsewhere, however, the courts came to allow witnesses from similar communities to testify. In this way a national rather than a purely local standard evolved.

In the following case, the local standard was overriden in favor of what might reasonably be expected of a nurse. The Georgia Court of Appeals held that failure of nurses to convey actual knowledge of an emergency room patient's heart condition and medication to the on-call physician showed such "an entire want of care and conscious indifference to consequences" that a jury could reasonably conclude that punitive damages were warranted.[8] The patient had been treated at the emergency room of the county hospital, and the physician on call had directed the care by telephone. The patient was discharged and later that morning had a cardiac arrest and subsequently died from complications arising out of a myocardial infarction. The jury returned a verdict in favor of the hospital, but the patient's children appealed, arguing that the jury should have been instructed to *the general standard of nursing care* rather than the "locality rule" standard. The locality rule suggested that in this particular community the nurse did act in accordance with reasonable standards of care. But the appeals court pointed out that nursing judgment should be a more universal standard, stating, "As the plaintiffs are questioning the professional judgment of defendant's nurses, rather than adequacy of services or facilities, the locality rule does not provide the appropriate standard of care." The court ruled that the nurses knew that the patient had a heart condition and had taken a nitroglycerin pill but failed to convey this information to the doctor or to obtain information about other medication being taken regularly. It stated that a physician may *reasonably* expect that experienced nurses will attend to their duties without detailed instruction: "A doctor has no responsibility to instruct or warn nurses with respect to performance of matters within the ordinary and customary duties of the nursing profession."[9]

The following example illustrates yet another way in which a national standard will override a local or hospital standard. In *HCA Health Services v. National Bank*,[10] a hospital attempted to escape liability for failing to conform to one of its policies by claiming the policy was "only a goal." Three nurses were working in a newborn nursery which consisted of three connecting rooms. Following report, one nurse worked with a baby in the admissions room and the other two nurses went to the second room, which contained 11 babies, 2 premature and 1 with jaundice. When the first nurse entered the third room, where there were 6 babies, she found that one infant had no heartbeat and had stopped breathing. Both the hospital's executive director and the nurse testified that the policy provided that a member of the nursery staff would be present in every room occupied by infants at all times. They argued that this was a goal, not a policy, but the court was not persuaded by the distinction. A physician testified that he believed the baby's problem would have been avoided if a nurse had been in the room with it, and the evidence indicated that the nurses had been on duty 1½ hours before the baby was found.

STANDARDS FOR LONG-TERM AND HOME CARE

Courts must also decide how standards apply to specific situations. For example, standards may differ regarding the issue of restraints. In the acute care hospital, the safety needs of the patient necessitate a high standard of care. On a short-term basis, it may be necessary to apply restraints, and a nurse in this situation is more likely to be held liable for failing to apply restraints to a patient who needs them than for applying restraints to a patient who may not have needed them. However, the very identical safety assessment in long-term care may result in a different outcome, since the courts recognize that applying restraints in a long-term care setting may be a lifelong issue for the resident. Therefore, there is more tolerance for failing to restrain the patient who may have fallen a number of times. Obviously the exact same analysis may occur in the home care setting: the same safety hazards may be apparent, but patients cannot be restrained in their own homes.

These considerations mean that standards of care must be applied to the specific facts of the case. The issue of control is different in the home care environment, and increasing numbers of cases are appearing that involve both long-term care and home care. These settings raise unique problems. In one extended care facility, for example, a mentally retarded woman chocked to death on a peanut butter sandwich despite orders not to give her peanut butter. Failure to adequately train personnel resulted in a settlement of over $50,000.[11] In one home care setting, a patient had had intestinal surgery. Two days after discharge, the nurse cleaning the wound at home found what she thought were maggots. The patient was readmitted and underwent surgery, but more maggots appeared, and she died eight months later of unrelated causes.

The prosecution charged that the surgeon failed to remove all dead tissue. The defense claimed that there were no maggots in hospital but that they might have developed from hot air in the home, and that they are not necessarily injurious because they feed only on dead tissue.[12] The defense won.

To date, not as many cases have been reported on home care as on acute in-patient care or extended nursing home care. This is not unexpected, since the courts tend to be many years behind current issues in health care. In *Jusko v. Lakeside Home Health Care Services*,[13] the plaintiff's decedent, age 83, suffered from Alzheimer's disease and was receiving nursing care at home. The plaintiff claimed that inappropriate care for a decubitus ulcer had caused it to progress. By the time the decedent was seen by a physician, she was forced to undergo immediate surgery because the ulcer had progressed down to the bone. During a second surgery to flap over the open wound, the patient suffered a myocardial infarction. A $75,000 settlement was paid by the defendants.

Some clinical high-risk indicators in home care that should be monitored are equipment failure, incorrect use of equipment by the client or the client's family, medication error, lack of follow-up by consultants as ordered and indicated, deviation by caregivers from agreed-upon plan of care, inappropriate or inadequate response by vendors, injury to the client, or exacerbation of the client's condition resulting from improperly controlled or maintained environmental conditions. Carefully screening clients before accepting them in home care will help avoid issues of abandonment.

NOTES

1. Fiesta, Janine, (1988). The law and liability: A guide for nurses (2nd ed., pp. 33-36) New York: Wiley.

2. Schneider v. Kings Highway Hospital Center, 490 N.E.2d 1221 (Ny. 1986).

3. Hartman v. Riverside Methodist Hospital, 577 N.E.2d 112 (Ohio 1989).

4. Utter v. United Hospital Center, Inc. 236 S.E. 2d 21 (W.Va. 1977).

5. Johnson, Kirk, (1989, January 6). Practice standards: MD's shield or plaintiff's spear? *American Medical News*.

6. Gallagher v. Detroit-Macomb Hospital, No. 95084 (Mich. 1988).

7. Harpster, Linda Marie. (1990, Spring). *Perspectives in Healthcare Risk Management*, p. 23.

8. Action-Kit, *Patient Care Law*, Horty-Springer, Nursing Standard of Care Increasing. (Nov. 1992) p.1.

9. Hodges v. Effingham County Hospital Authority, 355 S.E.2d 104 (Ga. App. 1987).

10. HCA Health Services v. National Bank, 745 S.W.2d 120 (Ark. 1988).

11. Blanenmeyer, N. New Concepts for the Handicapped Foundation, Inc. et al. (1991) *Medical Malpractice Verdicts, Settlements & Experts, 7* (4), 38.

12. Nagurney v. Bloch and Easton Hospital, Northampton, No. 1988 c3986, (1992). *Medical Malpractice Verdicts, Settlements & Experts, 8* (4).

13. Jusko v. Lakeside Home Health Care Services, 91-CV001274, Ohio. (1992). *Medical Malpractice Verdicts, Settlements & Experts, 8* (12).

Chapter 4

Responding Unwisely in a Short-Staffing Situation

Nursing shortages can present legal problems—and more pitfalls—for both the hospital and the nurse.

The reasons for these shortages are complex. Some have speculated that they are caused by low salaries, more job opportunities in other careers, and frustration with working conditions. Surveys indicate that hospitals should concentrate upon strategies that promote hospital culture over financial incentives.[1] Whatever their cause, nursing shortages may result in assignments which, at best, reduce the quality of nursing care received and, at worst, jeopardize the patients' safety. The recognition of nursing as a profession leaves nurses with a high degree of accountability for professional conduct.[2]

One problem may be the subjectivity of the nurse in determining what *short staffing* actually means. What is short staffing in one hospital is not necessarily the same as in another, depending upon the patient mix, the seriousness of the illnesses, and the availability and use of nonnursing personnel. National efforts to identify numerical ratios for the proper number of nurses per patient have met with mixed reviews. The nurse who is educationally prepared to care for the patient as an individual and to focus upon the total needs of the patient may be very frustrated by repeatedly scheduled assignments that do not allow time for this kind of comprehensive care. This repeated frustration is often cited by nurses who have left the nursing profession.

FLOATING POLICIES AND NURSES' LIABILITY

Among the frustrations caused by short staffing, floating policies rank high and can expose the nurse to liability. An extreme problem occurs when a nurse is asked to accept an assignment for which he or she is not prepared. For example, requiring a staff nurse to accept an assignment in a critical care unit when the nurse has never worked in such a unit poses a possible legal pitfall for the nurse: the indiscriminate *refusal to float*. Legal precedent suggests that nurses refuse such an assignment with great peril, since floating policies developed by hospitals have in general been upheld. For example, in *Francis v. Memorial General Hospital*,[3] a nurse was employed to work in the intensive care unit. Some time later, his supervisor told him to take temporary charge duty on the orthopedic unit. Even though floating was a hospital policy, he refused the assignment because he was unfamiliar with procedures on the unit and felt that he would jeopardize patient safety. He was suspended indefinitely. He also refused an offer to be oriented to the other unit. The court ruled for the hospital, holding that the hospital's floating policy was valid.

This kind of verdict is a reflection of the court's sympathy with the *patient's* standpoint. Since we are all potential patients, it would seem prudent for us to also understand this view of the health care world. If there are no other alternatives and the only option for patient care is the unprepared nurse, this is considered preferable to no nurse at all. Courts generally assume that every professional nurse is prepared to provide a basic level of patient care, including comfort measures, minimal assessment of needs, and intervention to meet safety needs. Nurses should also bear in mind that refusing an assignment places an additional burden on other nurses and in no way helps the patient. Therefore, prudent judgment suggests that the nurse should accept the assignment after making it clear to the nurse manager what his or her limitations and concerns are.

This is not to say, however, that nurses are always held liable in such situations. If floating is considered a matter of public concern—that is, potentially harmful to the public—it may be judged against public policy to penalize a nurse for refusing to float. Two cases will illustrate this issue. In *Churchill v. Waters*, a nurse who worked in an obstetrics department objected to the hospital's cross-training program and was supported in her criticism by the chief of the department. This allegedly offended hospital administrations, and she was fired for her negative attitude. The court condemned the hospital administration as being solely concerned with cost rather than care of patients. The review of the record provided very little, if any, education or training to prepare cross-trainees. The court stated that it would not condone an insubordinate or troublemaking employee but felt that nurse Churchill's actions fell far short of being a problem employee.[4] And in *Winkelman v. Beloit Memorial Hospital*,[5] the court looked at the training and orientation, or lack thereof, given to the nurses asked to float. It affirmed a jury verdict in favor of a nurse who was fired for refusing to work in another part of the hospital after working solely in the nursery for 15 years. Winkelman alleged that the hospital violated public policy as stated by the Wisconsin Board of Nursing, which defines negligence as including performing services as a registered nurse for which the nurse is not qualified by education, training, or experience. The court awarded her almost $40,000 in lost earnings. A dissenting judge thought it odd that Winkelman would feel unqualified to perform even menial tasks in another unit since she had a master's degree, teaching experience, and several years of nursing experience. The obstetrics nurse who did accept that assignment in place of Winkelman testified that there were things she felt uncomfortable doing and merely refused to do them; however, the nurse who accepted the assignment was not disciplined in any way for not doing the work she was uncomfortable with.[6]

FLOATING POLICIES AND HOSPITALS' LIABILITY

These last two examples raise the issue of the hospital's liability in these situations. It is clearly a management responsibility to provide proper staffing, both quality and quantity. Therefore, it is a management accountability problem as well as a potential corporate liability situation when management fails in this legal duty. Of course, even the best of hospitals may occasionally experience an unexpected short-staffing situation. The issue is much more serious when the problem continues and management fails to take any measures to correct it.

In order to fully understand the nurse's liability in a short-staffing situation, therefore, the principle of individual and professional accountability must be placed within the framework of the hospital's liability. The hospital that fails to maintain the level of nursing care required to provide safe, quality treatment may be held liable for any patient injuries that result under two separate legal theories, vicarious liability or respondeat superior, and corporate liability.[7]

Respondeat Superior (Vicarious Liability)

Under the doctrine of *respondeat superior,* the hospital is vicariously responsible for the acts of its employees simply because of the employer–employee relationship. An important implication of this principle is that the hospital will always be interested in defending its employees vigorously if they are named in malpractice cases. In *Horton v. Niagara Falls Memorial Medical Center*, the nurse in charge of an understaffed unit was held liable for failing to continuously supervise a confused patient who died in a fall.[8] The hospital was held liable not for its staffing decisions but because the charge nurse acted unreasonably and her actions were the proximate cause of the patient's death.

In this incident, the patient was discovered standing on his balcony, where he asked for a ladder. The charge nurse telephoned the patient's wife at home and asked if she could come and watch the patient. The wife responded that she would ask her mother (who lived closer to the hospital), but asked the charge nurse to watch her husband during the 10 minutes it would take her mother to get to the hospital. The charge nurse, citing staff shortages, said this would be impossible. The patient fell from the balcony during the 10-minute lapse in supervision and died, and the wife sued.

The court found the charge nurse negligent for failing to adequately supervise the patient, and the hospital ultimately liable, under the theory of respondeat superior, for the nurse's negligence. In ruling against the nurse, the court noted that there were orderlies from other areas of the hospital, as well as a new registered nurse assigned to the charge nurse for orientation, who could have watched the patient during the 10 minutes it would have taken the patient's mother-in-law to get to the hospital. The charge nurse also allowed another available aide to take a supper break during the time in question.

Corporate Liability

Under the theory of **corporate liability**, the hospital can be held liable for any injuries resulting from its own acts and omissions.[9] Because hospitals have a legal duty, under this theory, to provide the level of staffing needed to care safely for patients, they should be held liable for any injuries stemming from short staffing as long as the nurse did what would reasonably have been expected under the circumstances.[10]

The nurse working within the short-staffing situation can be held liable for his/her own inappropriate professional judgments. Allegations of failure to provide adequate numbers of staff and appropriate staff have begun to appear more frequently in malpractice cases, with varying verdicts. In *Zellar v. Tompkins Community Hospital*, the plaintiff fell while attempting to go to the bathroom and alleged that the hospital failed to maintain an adequate staff and that this resulted in failure to respond when she activated a call device for assistance.[11] In *Brooks v. Coliseum Park Hospital*, a 69-year-old hospital patient suffering from Alzheimer's disease suffered a broken hip when she was left unattended with the side rails of her bed down and later spilled her food and burned her thigh while eating unattended. In this case, the court held that the occurrences did not establish that the hospital had been negligent. In other words, it decided that failure to furnish constant attendance to a patient did not constitute negligence. The patient's physician had opposed the use of side rails for mentally confused patients, who might be injured in attempts to climb over them, and a psychiatric technician had encouraged the patient to feed herself as part of a program to help her reach a maximum level of functioning.[12]

The hospital's failure to provide 24-hour anesthesia service was an issue in *Herrington v. Hiller*.[13] The question was whether certified registered nurse anesthetists should be allowed to place epidural catheters in preparation for giving anesthesia. Because the hospital administration was not permitting this, the anesthesia group had refused to provide 24-hour service. The patient required an emergency caesarean section, and the delay in delivery resulted in severe brain damage to the baby. The physician settled but the hospital proceeded to trial. A second trial was required due to improperly excluded evidence and the ultimate decision was not reported.

In *Harrell v. Louis Smith Memorial Hospital*,[14] the plaintiff alleged that the hospital had failed to provide staff who were qualified to adequately diagnose and to treat myocardial infarction and had also failed to properly refer the patient to a facility capable of handling acute myocardial infarctions. The president of the hospital, in his deposition testimony, made several admissions which raised the issue of whether the emergency room was adequately staffed with competent and adequately instructed personnel.

As long as the nurse exercises reasonable professional judgment, establishes priorities, and communicates problems to his or her nursing supervisor, he or she will be defensible in a claim based upon short-staffing. In general, accountability follows control. If you are the individual with the ability to control the solution to the problem, then it follows that you should be accountable for failure to control. On the other hand, if you do not have the ability to control the situation, you should not be held accountable. Obviously, the individual staff nurse does not have the ability to solve the hospital's short-staffing problem. But the individual nurse's legal duty should be satisfied *as long as he or she fulfills the duty of communication.*

The standard of nursing practice requires that nurses practice as reasonably prudent nurses would practice under the same or similar circumstances. If the shortage of staff could not reasonably have been anticipated, nurses' documentation of the staffing situation under which they were functioning may help to determine that their actions were reasonable under the circumstances, a finding that could defeat a plaintiff's claim of negligence. Therefore, nurses should document their specific objections and submit those objections to the supervisor. This documentation will give the nurse manager and the risk manager specific information with which they can assess the potential risk posed by the hospital's level of staffing. If used appropriately, this information may help the hospital recognize the need to close units or to decrease the number of patients accepted.[15] No special form is necessary to provide this kind of documentation; a narrative memo, dated and signed, is sufficient. Of course, the nurse should always retain a copy of this memo to demonstrate that he or she has satisfied any individual liability.

NOTES

1. Wilkinson, Richard. (1987, November 20). *Hospitals*, p. 66.

2. Politis, Edith Kelly. (1983, Fall). Nurses' legal dilemma; When hospital staffing compromises professional standards. *University of San Francisco Law Review, 18.*

3. Francis v. Memorial General Hospital, 726 P.2d 852 (N. Mex. 1986).

4. Horty, John, Editor (1992, October/November). 'Floating' Policies Sink Two Hospitals, *Patient Care Law*, An Action-Kit Publication, 1–4.

5. Winkelman v. Beloit Memorial Hospital, 493 N.W. 2d 211 (Wis. 1992).

6. Horty, John, Editor (1992, October/November). 'Floating' Policies Sink Two Hospitals, *Patient Care Law*, An Action-Kit Publication, 1–4.

7. The nursing shortage: A liability threat. (1988, October). *Hospital Risk Control Update*, ECRI, 1.

8. 380 N.Y.S. 2d 116 (N.Y. 1976).

9. Thompson v. Nason Hospital, 591 A.2d 703 (1991).

10. Murphy, E.K. (1988). Assessing the nurse's liability exposure when short staffed. *AORN Journal*, 48 (1), 116–118.

11. Zellar v. Tompkins Community Hospital, 508 N.Y.S. 2d 84 (1987).

12. Brooks v. Coliseum Park Hospital, 369 S.E.2d 319 (Ga. App. 1988).

13. Herrington v. Hiller, No.88–2777 (5th Cr., Sept. 1989).

14. Harrell v. Louis Smith Memorial Hospital,. 397 S.E.2d 746 (Ga. App. 1990).

15. Cournoyer, Camelle Pellerin (1989). The nurse manager and the law. Rockville, MD: Aspen Publishers, Inc.

Chapter 5

Failing to Protect Oneself When Whistle-blowing

As many of the examples in the previous chapter have shown, accountability clearly exists in the nursing profession. However, when employees are unable to solve the problem (usually because they cannot control the circumstances), they must communicate significant information. How far does that duty of communication extend? What if an employee has communicated a problem to all significant persons of authority within the institution and the problem remains? When should the employee disclose information outside the institution?[1]

Whistle-blowing has been defined as a form of dissent resulting in public disclosure of perceived wrongdoing by members of one's own organization. In many of these situations, the employee has perceived serious harm to an individual or to the public, has reported these concerns to supervisors, and has exhausted all internal sources of remedy. The usual goal of a whistle-blower is prevention; changes are believed necessary to remedy a harmful situation. Occasionally the person who speaks out is an unhappy employee, but this seems to be the exception rather than the rule. A more typical whistle-blower is the dedicated, competent employee who is genuinely concerned about a situation perceived as harmful or potentially harmful to patients.

THE THREAT OF REPRISAL

In the absence of a clear-cut legal duty to report, the nurse who chooses to report or speak out may be a victim of retaliatory actions. Forms of reprisal may include dismissal, blacklisting, threats of violence, and general harassment.

There are many examples of reprisal. A nurse in California was fired for reporting what she believed was an "unethical" and "illegal" termination of respiratory and nutritional support to a patient. She was awarded $114,000 in civil damages.[2] In New York, a nurse is currently seeking $25 million for libel and conspiracy. She had informed the medical board that a physician documented on a medical record the performance of procedures that had not, in fact, been performed. She charged that after providing this information she was subjected to verbal, emotional, and psychological abuse.[3] In Wisconsin, a jury awarded $125,000 to a nurse who was fired after she organized staff opposition to what she said was mistreatment of minority patients.[4]

THE EMPLOYMENT-AT-WILL DOCTRINE

In the United States, under the **employment-at-will doctrine,** employers once had the authority to fire employees for any reason or no reason. Recently, state legislatures and the courts have limited this broad right. For example, employers may not discriminate on the basis of race, sex, religion, place of origin, or an employee's union activity.[5] Moreover, a bargaining agreement in a unionized hospital may limit management's ability to fire employees. Many union contracts require "just cause" for disciplining or discharging an employee. And if an employer states that an employee can be fired only "for cause" in a personnel handbook, this constitutes an implicit contract which takes precedence over the employment-at-will doctrine.

In April 1981, through the Whistle-blowers Protection Acts, Michigan became the first state to protect employees who expose illegal or dangerous employee activity.[6] This law provides that employees will be protected for exposing such activity. In California, a nurse CEO uncovered $3.25 million in fraudulent diagnostic related groups codes billed to Medicare. These coding mistakes always favored the hospital. She filed a whistle-blower lawsuit and received a percentage of what the government collected, $650,000.[7] More recently, applications of a **public policy exception** have attempted to limit the employment-at-will doctrine. If the nurse can demonstrate that the termination violates a clear and significant public policy, a legal action for wrongful discharge may be successful. Some activities protected by the public policy exception have included union membership, serving on a jury, or filing a workers' compensation claim. A nurse filing a worker's compensation claim should not be fired for asserting a legal right. Allowing such a termination would clearly discourage employees from exercising their legally protected rights.

In one case, the Arizona Supreme Court held that an employer may fire an employee at will for good cause or for no cause but not for "bad cause," such as complaining about a violation of public policy. The nurse claimed that she was discharged in part because she disapproved of her supervisors' and other employees' behavior, which violated the state's indecent exposure law.[8]

However, **patient advocacy** is not yet considered a public policy exception. Those claims of wrongful discharge which have been based on the public policy exception but which have been supported only by personal, moral, or ethical standards for patient care have not defeated the employer's right to fire under the employment-at-will doctrine. In Colorado, a head nurse was fired for her inability to follow staffing patterns and stay within budget. She sued the hospital for wrongful discharge, claiming that the preamble to the Nurse Practice Act required that she safeguard the patients' health and welfare. Her refusal to reduce her staff's overtime work was based on the belief that reducing the staff would jeopardize the health of the patients. The court refused to recognize the preamble to the Colorado Nurse Practice Act as a basis for the public policy exception to the employee-at-will doctrine.[9]

FREEDOM OF SPEECH

The First Amendment right to freedom of speech may offer some protection to whistle-blowers. To be entitled to constitutional protection, speech must relate to matters of "political, social, or other concern to the community."[10] In *Jones v. Memorial Hospital System*, a nurse who worked in the intensive care unit wrote an article describing conflicts between the wishes of terminally ill patients and their families and the orders of attending physicians. She signed her name to the article but did not implicate any specific physician or the hospital. She was fired and brought action against the hospital. The hospital argued that there was a legitimate basis for her termination other than the publication of her article. The court was not persuaded by this argument and focused upon whether her free speech right had been violated. It held that she was entitled to constitutional protection because the article was written on her own time, did not interfere with her work performance or with her employer's business, and was intended to inform the public on a controversial public issue.[11]

THE NEED FOR CAUTION

Although remedies remain somewhat limited, recent judicial opinions indicate significant movement toward protecting employees who question an employer's actions or policies. They show some recognition that employees who put the public's interest and welfare before that of their employer deserve society's support.[12] Nevertheless, although nurses are protected in public policy exceptions, the courts have not yet identified most patient care as falling within this domain. This fact means that nurses still need to be cautious, as the following cases illustrate.

Before deciding to take an issue outside the agency or institution, the nurse should consider these questions. Is there sufficient evidence to warrant action? A nurse making a serious accusation must have sufficient documentation to ensure fairness to the accused and to help maintain his or her own credibility. Has the nurse used all possible internal mechanisms? Following the usual channels of communication may not be sufficient: the nurse should also consider talking to the risk management and quality assurance systems. The decision to blow the whistle should not be made lightly because the disclosure will have serious ramifications for both the individual disclosing and the organization.

In *Wheeless v. Manning*,[13] a nurse wrote a proposal complaining about what the nurse alleged were matters of public interest: "wage discrimination" and low morale among the nurses, which could affect patient care. The nurse argued that this proposal was therefore protected by the First Amendment. The court disagreed, stating, "An examination of the proposal reveals that it is in essence an airing of employee grievances about wages, promotions, relations between the nurses and the director of nursing and employee input into policy changes." The court agreed that "a complaint about discrimination in wages based on race, sex or age would unquestionably involve matters of public interest." In this case, however, "the 'wage discrimination' protested by the proposal . . . was that the salaries for starting nurses with no experience were almost as high as those paid to more experienced nurses. This complaint that the salary structure was personally unfair to experienced nurses," said the court, "does not rise to the level of a matter of public concern."

In *Wright v. Shriners Hospital*, the assistant director of nursing was fired after criticizing the hospital during a survey visit. She had responded to questions by the survey team by describing communication problems between medical and nursing staffs which led to deteriorating morale among nursing personnel. The jury decided in favor of the nurse, but the appeals court rejected the trial judge's view that public policy was violated if the hospital fired her in reprisal for having criticized the hospital. In dissent, the chief justice expressed the view that given the public interest in good patient care, it must be the public policy of the state to protect, if not encourage, hospital employees who perceive and report potential detriments to patient care.[14] This case clearly shows that the issue is far from settled.

As stated before, the decision to refuse a work assignment may be based upon religious, ethical, or moral beliefs. For example, the nurse may find a course of treatment repugnant to his or her personal religious or ethical beliefs.[15] In the health care setting, the employee may argue that his or her refusal to administer treatment or participate in certain medical procedures, as a matter of conscience, is a right that public policy recognizes. Discharge for exercising that right would therefore be contrary to that mandate of public policy. Yet employers have no clear guidelines that might define what public policy actually may be at any moment in time. This means that, once again, a nurse must be very cautious in using such an argument.

In *Warthen v. Toms River Community Memorial Hospital*, the court found that a professional association's code of ethics does not represent a clear mandate of public policy. The nurse had refused to dialyze a terminally ill double-amputee patient because of her "moral, medical and philosophical objections" to performing the procedure.[16] The court stated that the nurses' code of ethics had defined a standard of conduct beneficial only to the individual nurse and not to the public at large. It affirmed that the most fundamental public policy is the preservation of life and that it would be virtually impossible to administer a hospital if each nurse or employee refused to carry out his or her duties based upon a personal private belief concerning the right to live.

In *Lampe v. Presbyterian Medical Center*,[17] the court found no public policy violation in the defendant's discharge of a licensed professional nurse for refusing to reduce nurse overtime in the intensive care unit. The plaintiff believed that reduced staffing would jeopardize patient care and relied upon a state regulation allowing the suspension of an individual's nursing license for conduct contrary to the health or safety of patients. The court declined to recognize the statute as embodying public policy, but rather found it merely a broad, general statement of policy not applicable to employment relationships.

All these examples show that in whistle-blowing, as in many other matters, nurses must proceed carefully and use their judgment if they hope to protect themselves in court.

NOTES

1. Fiesta, Janine. (1990, June). Whistleblowers : Heroes or stool pigeons? Part I. *Nursing Management, 21* (6), 16–17.

2. Fry, Sara. Whistle-blowing by nurses: A matter of ethics. *Nursing Outlook, 37* (1), 56.

3. Author Not Listed (1988). A Whistle-blowing RN seeks $25 million for "conspiracy." *American Journal of Nursing*, 20, 32.

4. Mallison, Mary B., RN, Editor-In-Chief (1992). Editorial: The great white lie hits a nerve. *American Journal of Nursing*, 92, 3,7.

5. Mallison, Mary B., RN, Editor-In-Chief (1992). Headlines. *American Journal of Nursing*, 92, (9) 9.

6. 42 U.S.C. 2000e; 29 U.S.C. 158 (a) (1) (4).

7. Michigan Comp. Laws, 15.361–5.369 (1980).

8. Wagenseller v. Scottsdale Memorial Hospital, 74 P.2d 412 (Ariz. 1984).

9. Lampe v. Presbyterian Medical Center, 590 P.2d 53 (Colo. 1978).

10. Horty, John, Editor (1986, October/November). Any "free speech" right has limits. *Patient Care Law*. An Action-Kit Publication, 1.

11. Jones v. Memorial Hospital System, 677 S.W.2d 221 (Tex. 1984).

12. Feliu, Alfred G. (1983 October). The risks of blowing the whistle, *American Journal of Nursing*, 83 (10), 1387-90.

13. Wheeless v. Manning, 682 F. Supp. 869 (Miss. 1987)

14. Wright v. Shriners Hospital, 589 N.E.2d 1241 (Mass. 1992).

15. Davis, Bruce G. (1986, October). Defining the employment rights of medical personnel within the parameters of personal conscience. *The Detroit College of Law Review*, 7.

16. Worthen v. Toms River Community Memorial Hospital, 488 A.2d 229 (N.J. 1985).

17. Lampe v. Presbyterian Medical Center, 590 P.2d 513 (Colo. 1979).

Chapter 6

Neglecting to Use Due Care in Physical Procedures

Several of the previous chapters have described situations in which the nurse's responsibility is ambiguous. In many physical procedures, however, the nurse's responsibility is clear, and failure to perform them correctly is a major pitfall. In fact, many nursing malpractice cases deal with a physical procedure from which the patient receives an injury. Obviously, the patient is more aware of these occurrences than those that deal with nonphysical aspects of care. Obviously, too, nurses who are patients are especially likely to recognize such malpractice events, and in many cases nurses are suing for these errors.

ERRORS IN SIMPLE PROCEDURES

Although people tend to think of malpractice cases as involving complex issues, it is, in fact, often the simplest tasks that result in an injury to the patient. The pitfall is in failing to exercise due care in all activities. In *Sanbrano v. Humana Hospital*, for example, an intravenous was inserted and not changed for 5 days; hospital policy required the line to be changed every 3 days. As a result, the patient developed a staph infection that invaded his hip prosthesis, and he
suffered three hip dislocations that required surgery each time. The jury awarded over $300,000.[1]

For one nurse, the simple task of removing tape from the patient's intravenous cite resulted in a malpractice case. In *Rutledge v. St. Anne's Hospital*,[2] the patient was hospitalized for a bladder infection and had an intravenous needle and plastic catheter in his left wrist. He alleged that the nurse tried three or four times to extract the catheter and the tape at the same time, but the tape remained adhered to his wrist and caused the catheter to move in a plunging direction while still inserted in his wrist, "wriggling" in a manner that caused extreme pain. He complained of the pain to the nurse, and on the morning after discharge, he noticed swelling in his wrist where the intravenous needle had been placed and called the hospital to report it. He was eventually diagnosed with chronic thrombophlebitis.

At trial, the director of nursing at a hospital, testifying as an expert for the plaintiff, stated that the standard of care for removing an intravenous required removing any dressings or tape dressings or tape securing the intravenous needle before removing the needle itself. The expert testifying for the defendant stated that she did not believe it was necessary to remove all tape from the catheter prior to removal. The nurse herself stated that although she had no independent memory of the patient, she did not believe she pulled on the catheter in the way the plaintiff described, had never had such an experience, and would have noted it on the patient's hospital chart. The jury decided in favor of the defense, and the patient appealed.

On appeal, the court held that the patient was denied a fair trial by the cumulative effect of the defense counsel's actions, which included improper statements in the closing argument. As the court stated, since

> the adversary system of litigation is alive and well, it does not require that counsel become gladiators prepared to fight to the death. Special care must be taken when reviewing a case such as this since it is difficult to determine the precise impact of this misconduct. There is not a magic number of instances that tilts the scales of justice. Counsel's conduct too often was beyond the margin of zealous advocacy and became acrimonious, overly contentious, and unswervingly determined to persuade the jury that plaintiff was attempting to conceal evidence without any evidentiary proof. The attorney's actions had the effect of denying the patient a fair trial.

It is unusual for a court to order a new trial because the proceedings are lengthy and costly. However, the court will always err on the side of fairness. And so, on the simple issue of removing tape, this nurse may need to go through two lengthy malpractice trials.

Many other simple procedures can lead to lawsuits. Urethral scarring due to unsuccessful insertion of a Foley catheter resulted in a 37-year-old patient receiving $161,900 in Missouri.[3] In New York, a patient, age 69, was admitted for eye surgery. Application of a hot water pack gave the patient second-degree burns to the buttocks and leg pain. The burn resulted in a disability which confined him to a wheelchair. The jury awarded $255,000.[4]

Because the administration of injections is usually part of the nurse's responsibility, liability for this simple procedure appears often in the nursing malpractice literature. In *Love v. Park Lane Medical Center* (1987),[5] a patient hospitalized for treatment of an ear infection needed two surgeries to debride the dead tissue caused by a negligently administered injection. The jury awarded $69,500. In *Fleming v. Baptist General Convention of Oklahoma*,[6] a patient with a history of chronic severe back pain received over 300 separate intramuscular injections during a 3-year period at a hospital emergency room. After a left thigh injection, the patient had gangrene. The allegation was that the injection was not given deeply enough; the jury awarded $60,000. In

Alabama, a 54-year-old patient received a jury award of $250,000 after experiencing a sciatic nerve injury. In her deposition, the nurse testified that she gave the injection in the right hip, but at trial she stated that she gave it in the left hip, which was in conformity with her note in the medical records.[7] (An important pitfall illustrated by this case is contradicting your own deposition testimony. For more on this, see Chapter 17.)

Simple failure to document the sites of injections has been a problem in nursing malpractice cases. In one unreported decision, an ambulatory surgery patient received two preoperative injections administered by two nurses—one in the left hip and one in the right. The patient sustained a *left* foot drop. Unfortunately, neither nurse had documented the location of the injection administered, and both nurses shared in the cost of the settlement. In general, specific documentation such as this is often missing in malpractice uses. It is not unusual to find that nurses are specifically named as defendants in these types of cases.

MEDICATION ERRORS

All the perfect systems in the world cannot prevent all errors as long as there is a human component present. So it is with medication errors. Fortunately, the majority of errors do not result in malpractice cases because most errors do not cause an injury. Sometimes nurses who administer the wrong medication say to the patient, "I was negligent; I gave you the wrong drug" (or wrong amount). In fact, the nurse was *not* negligent according to the technical legal definition of malpractice or professional negligence unless harm or injury occurred to the patient. Nevertheless, medication errors are common and can have outcomes as serious as death. Some experts estimate that the number of such errors in the United States could be as high as $15 billion a year.[8] The average patient receives 10 different drugs during a hospitalization.[9] Because of the number and variety of individuals involved in the administration of medications, each dose of a drug presents multiple opportunities for error.[10] According to the American Society of Hospital Pharmacists, one patient per day per hospital will experience a medication error.[11]

Nurses are expected to know the correct dosage range of medications, the side-effects of drugs, and any clinical information about a drug that might have an impact upon the patient. In other words, they are the *final check and balance* for the medication administration system. This means that finding the wrong drug in the patient's medication area and removing it before it is administered is practicing sound risk management.

In the following case, the nurse's liability was clear. A 44-year-old patient was being treated for psychiatric disorders. Her treatment included long-term use of Nardil. A licensed practical nurse at the facility administered a dose of Triaminicol, which was contraindicated when used with Nardil and caused the patient to develop a stroke. Liability in administering the medication was admitted by the defendant, and a settlement of $150,000 was reached.[12]

Drug overdoses can also be a problem. In Connecticut, a 40-year-old nurse was hospitalized to undergo cardiac bypass surgery on an urgent basis. The nurse had had a previous bypass 10 years earlier. While waiting for surgery, a nurse administered a heparin overdose, which necessitated that the surgery be rescheduled for 5 days later. The decedent suffered a massive myocardial infarction and died 2 days before the scheduled surgery.[13]

Although most medication error cases involve a drug overdose or the wrong drug to the wrong patient, it is important to note that the omission of a drug may also produce a liability situation. In *Schultz v. Oak Park Hospital*,[14] the jury awarded $1 million against the hospital when an undiagnosed diabetic claimed that an additional amputation was required because hospital personnel failed to administer prescribed Penicillin for gangrene; at least, the medical record did not indicate that the medication was administered. Although the absence of documentation is not a fatal error in malpractice cases, this case shows that since administered medications should be charted, the failure to chart a medication might well suggest that it was not, in fact, administered.

In some cases, of course, such an assumption benefits the health care provider. In one case, an obese woman in her sixties who had heart disease and required an aortic valve replacement died in the recovery room. The plaintiffs claimed that an overdose of Levophed given in the recovery room by the nursing staff caused cerebral edema and death. There were no written orders for Levophed. The defendants contended that oral orders for drugs were within the standard of care and that there was no overdose of Levophed given. The physician said death was idiopathic from the high-risk surgery. A defense verdict was returned.[15]

WHAT MIGHT HAPPEN IN COURT

The majority of claims reported by the Risk Management Foundation of the Harvard Medical Institutions allege some physician error such as improper management of the medication regimen. The clear paper trail associated with medication prescription, dispensing, and administration makes medication-related claims particularly difficult to defend, even when direct causation is not proven. A lay jury can readily comprehend, for example, that a patient should not have received 10 times the ordered dose of medication. In such cases, expert witness testimony and other factors pointing to an appropriate level, and no connection to any damages, may be overshadowed by the medication error.

To illustrate, a 54-year-old patient underwent a total hysterectomy with removal of ovaries and fallopian tubes because of ovarian cancer. The oncologist who developed the protocols for the use of Leukeran as a chemotherapeutic agent for ovarian cancer treated the patient on this drug. During the almost 10 years that the patient was on Leukeran, her blood counts began to fall and she was eventually diagnosed with leukemia. The family claimed Leukeran was responsible for the leukemia and should not have been used. Since the family refused an autopsy, the cause of death was in dispute; nevertheless, the jury returned a $1,750,000 verdict.[16] In the absence of an autopsy, it is often difficult to determine the cause of death as it relates to malpractice allegations. In this case, the cause was placed on medication error.

Deaths or cardiac arrests may result from accidental free flow of medication. An uncontrolled flow of medication from the intravenous bag through tubing to the patient can also occur when the tubing is improperly removed from the pump. Although some pumps are designed with a mechanism that automatically cuts off the flow if the tubing is pulled out of the pump, other devices require health care workers to shut the flow manually with a safety clamp.

THE ROLE OF MANAGEMENT

As the nurse moves away from the patient's bedside, liability exposure for malpractice decreases. However, as the nurse moves into management positions, the liability exposure for failing to make reasonable management decisions and the liability for personnel issues increases. Nurses can be held liable for failing to teach employees and failing to communicate as well as for other nonphysical activities. The patient is often not aware of these examples of negligence. Sometimes patients do not sue because they do not know they have been malpracticed upon!

In general, damages in a malpractice case are meant to be compensatory in nature. Occasionally, however, a punitive damage award is allowed when the conduct of the defendants is outrageous: totally beyond the boundaries of what is considered reasonable. (For more information on punitive damages, see Chapter 18.)

Because chemotherapeutic agents can be very caustic, these intravenous administration cases may result in serious injuries and large damage awards. In *Latham v. Southwest Detroit Hospital and Jane Doe,* the patient, age 63, was receiving chemotherapy and had a subcutaneous infiltration that necessitated multiple plastic surgeries. She alleged that the defendant nurse was negligent in allowing the needle to go subcutaneous and that the hospital was negligent in failing to properly treat her hand. The defendants contended that the nurse checked for good blood flow before administering the chemicals and the plaintiff reached for a telephone during the administration of the drugs, causing the needle to go subcutaneous. According to the defendants, nothing could have been done to alter the outcome. The jury returned a $500,000 verdict, but also assessed 5% comparative negligence against the plaintiff because the nurse had instructed the plaintiff to treat the hand by soaking it in hot water, and the plaintiff attempted that treatment for 6 days and failed to seek medical care as the condition worsened.[17]

In *Summerville v. Volk,*[18] a 9-month-old became ill with a stomach virus. Because the baby became dehydrated, he was admitted and intravenous solutions were ordered at 150 cc per hour for 6 hours with one-quarter normal saline solution. During the next 5 hours, the child's condition deteriorated. He became lethargic, arrested, and died. The parents claimed that excessive amounts of fluid caused the brain to swell and the brain stem to herniate. They alleged that nurses lacked the proper training to care for an infant and failed to recognize signs of deterioration and to report these to the physician. The jury awarded $1.4 million, including $5,000 in punitive damages.

Admitting children to the hospital for intravenous fluids because they are dehydrated is not an unusual event and in fact is probably one of the most common reasons for children requiring hospitalization. In *McNeal v. Anne Arundel General Hospital,*[19] an intravenous placed in a child's foot extravasated and caused necrotic tissue. Extensive grafting was necessary and scarring remained. The focal issue was how long the intravenous had remained in the child's foot without being checked. The medical records were confusing, with one entry indicating that the child was left unattended for 2 hours with the ankle wrapped and another entry indicating he was left unattended for 4 hours with no wrapping. A settlement of $75,000 was reached prior to the involvement of a defense attorney.

The measurement of whether the nurse was negligent in a malpractice case is always whether he or she acted as a reasonable professional. In Georgia, it was alleged that a nurse had been negligent in the site selection for and the administration of an intravenous injection. The jury was instructed that a nurse, was not required to exercise the specialized technique or understanding of a skilled physician or surgeon in the care or treatment of a patient, but only the reasonable degree of care and skill ordinarily exercised by nurses generally under similar conditions and surrounding circumstances.

Under the doctrine of vicarious liability (discussed in Chapter 4), either the physician or the hospital may be held partially accountable for a medication error. In a Montana case, a nurse anesthetist was found negligent in giving too much Pavulon to a woman during her hysterectomy and then disconnecting the respirator too soon. She had been given 6 mg of Pavulon rather than 3.6. The gynecologist claimed that the decedent had taken an overdose of prescribed antidepressants prior to surgery. The hospital pathologist ruled death due to overdose of anti-depressants. The state crime lab toxicologist testified that methods used to sample blood and tissue biased the results and this together with lack of knowledge about how this type of drug reacts after death made the toxicology results unreliable. The jury returned a $302,461 verdict, finding the nurse anesthetist negligent and the physician not personally negligent but responsible for the nurse's negligence.[20]

The pharmacy can also be held liable for its acts of negligence. Sometimes a medication is supplied to the clinical area and it is impossible for the nurse to know that the dosage is incorrect or that the wrong medication has been supplied. In one case, when an infant received an 88% solution of potassium chloride rather than 8%, a $425,000 settlement was reached. The infant, who was born with respiratory distress, had brain damage and cerebral palsy. The defendant claimed the injury was congenital. The error was blamed on the pharmacy computer.[21]

It is often difficult for the injured plaintiff to prove that the breach of duty by the defendant actually caused the injury suffered. The use of experts may be necessary. In *Jones v. Rapides General Hospital*[22] the patient met the burden of proving that a hospital technician had breached the standard of care when she attempted multiple venipuncture on her arm with the same needle, and that this breach was the cause of the gas gangrene infection. Both the patient's expert witness and the technician who had performed the venipuncture had testified that, once a needle had come into contact with a patient's skin, it was considered contaminated, since it is impossible to completely sterilize the human skin. The patient's expert witness also stated that the sole way the patient could have contracted the extensive infection found deep in her arm was by transmission of bacteria directly into the arm by the needle. Given the physical evidence of multiple attempts on the arm, the expert had concluded that, more probably than not, multiple venipuncture had been the cause of the infection.

On the other hand, for some situations the courts have ruled that an expert witness is not necessary. In *Welte v. Mercy Hospital*,[23] the patient was admitted for correction of a deviated septum. The defendant anesthesiologist administered an intravenous anesthetic, injection sodium Pentothal into the intravenous line that had been placed by a nurse, but the patient did not become unconscious. He then noticed a swelling near the point where the intravenous had been inserted. The patient suffered first-, second-, and third-degree burns from infiltration by the drug into the tissues surrounding the vein. He was not able to find an expert but argued that the doctrine or **res ipsa loquitur** ("the thing speaks for itself") should apply. The Iowa Supreme Court agreed and held that the insertion of an intravenous line was within the common experience of laypersons and that expert testimony was not required to establish deviation from the standard of care.

Sometimes suing the incorrect defendants (a nonresponsible party) may result in a dismissal of the claim. Many plaintiffs' attorneys in malpractice cases are not experienced in malpractice litigation. Since there is no legal requirement in most jurisdictions to have the case evaluated medically before the lawsuit is initiated, the inexperienced attorney may make an error of judgment.

This happened in *Blanchard v. County of Sonoma, Tomasin, M.D., Smith, M.D., and Keefer, M.D.*[24] The patient, a 24-year-old male, underwent surgery to repair a fractured left femur. During surgery, he sustained a burn from a warm intravenous bag for support under his left arm. He contended that all personnel in the operating room were liable under the doctrine of res ipsa loquitur. The nurse, who was not sued, testified that she retrieved the bag from an anteroom, brought it into the operating room, and handed it to a doctor, but she did not recall which doctor asked for the bag or to which doctor she handed it. The defendant physicians contended that none of them had touched the bag and had no reason to know its temperature. They argued that res ipsa loquitur did not apply because the only parties that had control of the bag causing the injury were the hospital and the nurse, and they had been released from the case.

In this case, then, although the patient suffered a third-degree burn to his left underarm approximately 5 by 10 inches in size and surgery was required for a skin graft, the defendants were granted a **nonsuit** because nonresponsible parties had been sued. An experienced malpractice attorney would have had the case reviewed prior to filing and would have used the services of a nurse to review the medical record and the care given to the patient.

CAUSES AND SOLUTIONS

Why do errors occur, and what can be done about them? Low-level, semi-automatic behavior is used for many routine daily activities, but *inappropriate persistence* of automatic behavior leads to slips, or errors of implementation. For example, in the past, anesthesiologists have inadvertently attached a tank containing a gas other than oxygen to the oxygen nozzle. This problem was solved by making the oxygen yoke unique, so that only another oxygen tank could be fitted to it. In contrast, higher level functioning is employed in new or nonstereotypic situations where decisions are needed. This requires conscious effort and is much slower than low-level, semiautomatic behavior. Errors of high-level functioning, decision-making errors, or errors of intention have been called "mistakes." It is more difficult to prevent "mistakes" than to prevent "errors."

Inexperience is a common cause of medication mistakes. In the operating room, surgeons rely upon the accuracy of the solutions provided by the staff: they are not responsible for independently verifying the medications. In one case the physician requested a 3% to 5% solution of acetic acid for surgery to remove vaginal warts, but a solution of over 30% was used, and the patient needed skin grafts. The plaintiff alleged that the nurses were not trained in this procedure.[25]

In another case, a doctor ordered an intravenous infusion of amphotericin B for an intensive care patient with fungal sepsis. He also ordered aspirin and corticosteroids. Unfortunately, he omitted the administration route for aspirin: the order simply read, "aspirin grs. X and Methylprednisolone 125 mg. IV." As the nurse processed the order, she assumed she was supposed to give the aspirin intravenously. To be sure, she asked a more experience nurse how it should be given. The other nurse knew that the patient had a nasogastric tube, so she told the new nurse to crush the tablets and mix them with water. The new nurse did this and then attempted to inject the solution intravenously. She realized she made an error when the intravenous central line became clogged.[26] Better communication as well as more experience would have prevented this mistake. (For more on communication, see Chapter 14.)

Physicians' illegible handwriting is a serious problem that contributes to medication errors. In some hospitals physicians have been identified through the quality assurance process as illegibility offenders and are now required as a condition of their privileges to print their orders and progress notes. In one hospital, nurses decided as a department, with the support of the medical staff, that they would no longer devote hours of valuable patient care delivery time to tracking down doctors to clarify orders. They adopted a policy that prohibited nurses from clarifying such orders by telephone. Nurses were allowed only to call the physician and state that an illegible order existed; the physician was then required to return to the unit and rewrite the order. No telephone orders were permitted for clarification purposes. (Telephone conversations are a definite source of liability exposure since telephone orders can be ambiguous.)

Quality experts outside the health care delivery system believe that the most common cause of quality problems is the production process itself, not the individuals operating within it.[27] According to this theory, the assignment of responsibility for accidents is usually misplaced. Although "human error" may have occurred, the root cause is a defect in the design of the system that permitted a relatively minor operator error to result in an accident. For example, a physician who fails to follow up an important lab result when it becomes available several days later in the clinic or office can be faulted, but a properly designed system would prevent this oversight.

An important aspect of risk management is therefore evaluating all systems to prevent a breakdown before patients are injured. Any potential for patient injury should be identified early, as the following case shows. An infant with a congenital heart defect suffered an arrest after being taken from a monitor and being removed from the oxygen hood. The patient's mother claimed that the nurses took the child out of the oxygen hood and removed the monitor against the physician's orders and also that abnormal vital signs of inconsolable crying and irritability and abnormal pulse, respiration, and heart rate were ignored. The nurses testified that the physician never ordered the monitor and gave his approval to remove the child from the hood. They also claimed that they called the resident physician about the abnormal vital signs, but there was no response before the arrest occurred. The admitting physician and resident denied this. The court ordered the quality assurance investigation report to be produced, which showed that the nurse stated 3 days after the incident that the monitor was removed because of the high heart rate, which was causing the alarm to go off continuously. The jury awarded over $10 million against the hospital.

It is impossible to eliminate all errors and to perfectly design all systems, but some interventions help reduce drug-related adverse events by catching errors before medications are given to patients. One promising approach involves using the hospital computer system to check for drug errors. This may allow allergies to be picked up, as well as a physician to order theophylline for a patient who already has a high blood level.

Another solution is to encourage patients and families to double-check the administration of medications they are taking in the hospital. Patients and families could be given a list of all the drugs the patient is receiving.[28] Health care providers sometimes fail to listen to patient families, who do *sometimes* know what they are talking about, and failing to listen is a pitfall.

When errors are made, they should be reported. Nurses have an ethical and a professional obligation to report their own errors and in general do an exemplary job of meeting this responsibility. *Incident reports* (see Chapter 17) are a risk management reporting tool, and nurses should report medication errors through this vehicle. They should not be treated punitively for reporting incidents, since the goal of the incident reporting process is prevention, not punishment.

Abbreviations are also a problem. Do not use *U* for *unit*. A poorly written *U* looks like an *O*, and *6U* of regular insulin easily is misread as *60*. Ask physicians not to use trailing zeros. Decimals may not land on the line, and *1.0* easily becomes *10*.

In addition, nurses should be careful with products that look alike; do not assume anything. The same principles apply here as when you come home from the grocery store with a can of tuna in oil and you really wanted to buy tuna in water.

As the next chapter will discuss in more detail, it is also imperative to check technical systems. The increased use of intravenous medications and of chemotherapy has resulted in a corresponding increase in cases filed due to injury sustained by the patients receiving treatment. A recent article in *Modern Healthcare* states that as many as half of the $500,000 electronic infusion devices used at U.S. hospitals could accidentally release too much medication and should be replaced.[29]

NOTES

1. Sanbrano v. Humana Hospital, No. 52-17-82. (1992). *Medical Malpractice Verdicts, Settlements & Experts, 8* (11), 33.

2. Ruttledge v. St. Anne's Hospital, 595 N.E.2d 1165 (Ill. 1992).

3. Williams v. Lee's Summit Community Hospital. (1991). *Medical Malpractice Verdicts, Settlements & Experts, 7* (1), 32.

4. Rossy v. New York Eye and Ear Hospital. (1991). *Medical Malpractice Verdicts. Settlements & Experts, 7* (4), 29.

5. Love v. Park Lane Medical Center, 737 S.W.2d 720 (Mo. 1987).

6. Fleming v. Baptist General Convention of Oklahoma, 742 P.2d 1087 (Okla. 1987).

7. Long v. St. Vincent's Hospital, CV-86-6832. (1990). *Medical Malpractice Verdicts, Settlements & Experts, 6* (5), 7.

8. Soares, M.S., (1992). The pharmacist's role in risk management. *Perspective in Healthcare Risk Management: The American Society for Healthcare Risk Management of the American Hospital Association, 12* (3), 2-5.

9. Jick, H. (1984). Adverse drug reactions: The magnitude of the problem. *Journal of Allergy Clinical Immunology, 74,* 555–557.

10. Bates, David W. (1991). Drugs, adverse events and claims. *Forum, 12* (6), 3-5.

11. Bell, Clark W. Hospitals should act on the problem of medication errors, not avoid the issue. Modern Healthcare, Nov. 18, 1991, p.32.

12. Fountain v. Psychiatric Institute of America, d/b/a/ Highland Hospital et al., No. 89-CVS-4179 (N.C. 1991).

13. Mitchell v. Hartford Hospital No. CV-91-05000812. (1993). *Medical Malpractice Verdicts. Settlements & Experts, 9* (2), 5.

14. Schultz v. Oak Park Hospital. (1992). *Medical Malpractice Verdicts. Settlements & Experts, 8* (11), 32.

15. McGrath et al. v. Sharp Memorial Hospital et al., No. 628601.(1992). *Medical Malpractice Verdicts. Settlements & Experts, 8* (12), 20.

16. Jablonski v. Masterson, No. 87-L6573. (1993). *Medical Malpractice Verdicts. Settlements & Experts, 9* (2), 37-38.

17. Latham v. Southwest Detroit Hospital. (1991). *Medical Malpractice Verdicts. Settlements & Experts, 7* (1), 45.

18. Summerville v. Volk. 3 (1992). *Medical Malpractice Verdicts. Settlements & Experts, 8* (10), 49.

19. McNeal v. Anne Arundel General Hospital. (1990). *Medical Malpractice Verdicts, Settlements & Experts, 6* (10), 26.

20. Spicher v. Miller, Havre Clinic et al., No. DV-88179. (1991). *Medical Malpractice Verdicts, Settlements & Experts, 7* (12), 6.

21. Whitlock v. The Regents of the University of California, No. 514905. (1992). *Medical Malpractice Verdicts, Settlements & Experts, 8* (8), 55-56.

22. Jones v. Rapides General Hospital, 598 So.2d 619 (La. 1992).

23. Welte v. Mercy Hospital, 482 N.W.2d 437 (Iowa 1992).

24. Blanchard v. County of Sonoma, Tomasin, M.D., Smith, M.D., and Keefer, M.D., *Medical Malpractice Verdicts, Settlements & Experts, 7* (1), 45.

25. Goering v. John C. Lincoln and Michael Kopiec, M.D., No. CV89-24889. (1991). *Medical Malpractice Verdicts, Settlements & Experts, 7* (11), 29.

26. Cohen, Michael R. (1992). Medication errors: Help New Nurses Avoid Making Errors. *Nursing '92, 22* (4), 21.

27. Deming, W.E. (1986). *Out of the Crisis.* (Cambridge, MIT-CAES).

28. Author unnamed (1992). Medication errors: High liability and price for hospitals. *Hospital Risk Management,14* (10), 129.

29. Wagner, Mary (1992, June 8) Half of Infusion Pumps Could Cause Mishaps, Modern Healthcare, p.4.

hapter

7

Not Checking
Equipment

Contrary to what many nurses believe, high-tech units, such as the intensive care unit, do not see the most nursing negligence suits.[1] The majority of hospital injuries occur in areas such as the medical–surgical unit, where falls are the number one reason a nurse will find herself or himself in the courtroom (see Chapter 1). Nevertheless, equipment is a definite source of liability exposure for the nurse in any clinical area, such as a critical care unit, that uses a large volume of devices. Equipment problems may occur anywhere in the health care delivery system—acute in-patient, ambulatory care, long-term care, or home care—but they are most common in the operating room. Sometimes the problem is one of safety; in other instances, the equipment fails to function as it should.

Nurses at the bedside are usually in the best position to evaluate whether a device is functioning. One pitfall is that nurses *fail to trust their own instincts* and use a device even when they have misgivings about it. If a piece of equipment is in question, the nurse should remove the item from use and have it reviewed by the appropriate individual, either biomedical engineering or others in the hospital who have this designated responsibility.

MANUFACTURER AND DISTRIBUTOR LIABILITY

Once a patient is injured, the risk manager should be notified, who may determine that the equipment should be sent out for an *independent review.* Such a review is important because it frequently provides defensibility in a malpractice lawsuit. Although sending the product to the manufacturer is not an uncommon procedure, this is not the best option for malpractice protection and damage control, since the manufacturer in a products liability case will allege that it was the user's (doctor's, nurse's) misuse of the product that actually caused the patient's injury, rather than a defective product.

The rationale behind the doctrine of **strict liability** or **products liability** is that those who profit from the sale or distribution of a product should bear the financial burden of an undetectable product defect. Some courts have held that the doctrine does not apply to a health care provider, such as a hospital, since the primary function of a hospital is providing medical services, not selling products or equipment.[2] However, other court decisions suggest that since the patient has no actual choice as to what equipment will be used, the hospital should be held to a higher standard of care.

Products liability does mean that manufacturers can be held at least partially liable for equipment errors. In one case, a 20-year-old man underwent brain surgery during which the drill malfunctioned and plunged into his head, causing him permanent paralysis and blindness. He asserted that the drill had not been properly cleaned and assembled before use and that its design was defective. He also alleged that the warnings accompanying the drill were inadequate. The manufacturer blamed the incident on the hospital's failure to clean the drill for months before surgery. The jury awarded the plaintiff $6 million, finding the hospital 67% and the manufacturer 33% negligent.[3]

Distributors can also be held liable. For example, the North Dakota Supreme Court held that a clinic and a distributor of a high-intensity surgical lamp were both liable for damages as a result of burns an infant sustained from the lamp. The 3-month-old infant was hospitalized for congestive heart failure and underwent a cardiac catheterization. During this procedure, a high-intensity lamp was used to illuminate the area. Prior to the surgery, a technician had informed the physician that the lamp had broken during an emergency procedure the previous evening; however, the physician did not know that the heat protection filter had fallen off. The infant was exposed to the lamp for approximately 15 minutes and received second- and third-degree burns in the groin area and inner thigh. She underwent plastic surgery and had permanent scars. The jury awarded $163,291.98 and found the clinic 60% negligent and the distributor 40% negligent. The court found sufficient evidence that the distributor was negligent for failing to warn of the dangers in using the lamp without its heat protection filter because it was foreseeable that the housing of the lamp would be removed accidentally.[4]

COMMON SOURCES OF ERROR

Unfamiliarity with New Equipment

The cases involving equipment deal with every device that is used in the health care delivery system, from the most simple to the most complex. As each new piece of equipment appears, a new liability exposure also appears. With any new piece of equipment, therefore, it is extremely important that everyone understand what needs to be done before the equipment is first used. In a recent case, a 6-figure settlement was reached with a physician and a confidential settlement with the hospital when a woman died after suffering an arrest during a procedure to remove the inside lining of the uterus with a laser. The allegation was that the laser nurse provided the incorrect fiber. The surgeon had not discussed the laser chosen and had not inspected or identified the laser.[5]

An extremely serious series of cases occurred in the late 1980s when several pediatric patients around the United States were fatally crushed by an electric hospital bed. The Hill-Rom bed had a walk-away "down" control that allowed the bed to descend automatically to its lowest position when activated by a control switch. In 1989, a hospital center acknowledged that it had not acted on a 1987 warning from the hospital bed manufacturer to deactivate the automatic feature.[6]

In a 1990 case a New York hospital furnished a physician with a defective catheter that had been manufactured by the Bard Company and was the subject of two separate recalls. The court said there was no need for medical expert testimony regarding the standard of care in a case that dealt with administrative rather than medical issues. Clinical expertise is not required to decide a management or administrative matter. The jury awarded $75,000.[7]

Faulty Use of Equipment

Sometimes injury happens because of basic errors in using a piece of equipment. In Minnesota, a $2.1 million settlement occurred when a 6-year-old, following surgery for a congenital heart defect, was without oxygen because a nurse had disconnected a respirator hose and reconnected it to the wrong port on the respirator machine. Depositions also revealed that the nurse had disabled the alarm system. At the time of the child's discharge from the hospital, the parents were informed that the hospital would not charge them for his treatment, but they were sent a bill for approximately $50,000, and another portion of the bill was sent to a collection agency.[8]

Not all patients who should receive compensation do! In another case, a child with severe congenital defects was abandoned by her parents and was under care of a guardian and the state. She died almost instantly when a nurse at the hospital, intending to insert heart monitor leads into a heart monitor machine, mistakenly plugged them into a power cord which was plugged into a wall socket. The jury returned a defense verdict after learning that the child's father, who initiated the lawsuit, had left the state to avoid warrants for his arrest.[9]

In a Pennsylvania case, the patient was placed on the ventilator in an intensive care unit after an automobile accident. When a disconnect occurred, the alarms did not ring because they were allegedly not set.

The patient suffered hypoxic brain injury and went into a persistent vegetative state. The jury awarded $6.5 million.[10]

Reuse of Materials

Reuse of materials has also been an issue in some cases. One example was a 45-year-old man admitted to a hospital for diagnostic tests to determine the cause of chest pain. A doctor tried to perform an angiography, but two arterial catheters failed to work. An assistant found another disposable catheter, and the doctor inserted it into the patient's bronchial artery. During the procedure the 4-inch tip of the catheter broke off. X-rays showed that the tip had traveled to the patient's abdomen, but the surgeons were unable to find it; hours later it was found in the thigh and removed. As a result of this injury, the patient was unable to return to work. Pretrial discovery revealed that the catheter was 10 years old and had been sterilized and reused at least 19 times, in spite of manufacturer's warnings. The manufacturer had discontinued production of that particular catheter 10 years earlier, and when a company representative visited the hospital 2 years later to collect the old catheters, the hospital said it had none. After the incident, 53 of that type of catheter were found at the hospital. The manufacturer settled before trial for $100,000, and the jury awarded compensatory damages against the hospital and doctor, and an additional $750,000 in punitive damages against the hospital alone.[11]

HOW TO AVOID LIABILITY

Appropriate maintenance of devices and equipment will provide defensibility in many cases. We are not guaranteers of safety, and the courts understand that despite all reasonable measures, patients are injured. For example, in Ohio, a woman who caught her fingers in the sliding door at the hospital claimed that guards should have been in place to prevent her soft tissue injuries. The jury accepted the hospital's defense that it had properly maintained its premises.[12]

When injuries do occur, it is extremely important to *retain the piece of equipment in question.* In Maryland, the jury awarded $628,000 to a patient because a hospital bed had collapsed. The court allowed the jury to *infer* negligence because the bed was not available for inspection.[13] In another case, a patient recovering from herniated disc surgery found her bed folding into a V, causing her pain and allegedly requiring her second surgical procedure. The previous occupant of the bed testified that she had a similar experience but that hospital personnel had refused to change or repair the bed. Hospital maintenance records were unclear concerning whether the bed had been repaired. The hospital failed to segregate the bed after the incident, and it was not available for testing or inspection. The manufacturer's manual noted in an "injury warning" that beds of this model were known to operate in a phantom manner for an unknown reason. The head of the maintenance department testified that the bed could not move electronically in the precise way alleged and had never done so, to his knowledge. The jury decided in favor of the hospital.[14]

Hospital maintenance records become very important to the defense of such cases. The manufacturer's pamphlet describing the appropriate use of the equipment should be retained. In addition, since nursing is frequently involved in staff orientation and training, records verifying attendance and training should be kept as long as necessary, depending upon the state regulations and the statute of limitations, which defines the length of time during which suits can be initiated for an injury. Since the statute may be very lengthy in some states, this documentation should not be discarded without the approval of the risk manager.

NOTES

1. Cushing, M. Maureen. (1992, July). Back to (PACU) Basics. American Journal of Nursing, 7, 21.

2. North Miami General Hospital v. Goldberg, No. 87-337 (Fla. App. Ct. Feb. 23, 1983).

3. Schmutz v. Boulder Community Hospital and Codman & Shurtleff, Inc. (1992). Medical Malpractice Verdicts, Settlements & Experts, 8 (10), 31.

4. Witthauer v. Burkhart Roentgen, 467 N.W.439, (1991).

5. Starkey v. Meridia Hillcrest Hospital, No. 193332. (1992). Medical Malpractice Verdicts, Settlements & Experts, 8 (11), 29.

6. Author not listed, (1989). Electric beds: Another child dies. ECRI, 7.

7. Pearce v. Feinstein, Genesee Hospital, 754 F. Supp. 308 (N.Y. 1990).

8. Mele v. St. Mary's Hospital of Rochester, Minnesota and Mayo Foundation, CV-3-87-818. (1991). Medical Malpractice Verdicts, Settlements & Experts, 7 (10), 32.

9. Stark v. Childrens Orthopedic Hospital and Medical Center, No. 87-2-12416-9. (1990). Medical Malpractice Verdicts, Settlements & Experts, 6 (10), 28.

10. Wagner v. York Hospital, 608 A.2d 496 (Pa. 1992).

11. Mosely v. Castillo, No. 79-21313 (Fla.1981).

12. Eiland v. St. Elizabeth Hospital v. Stanley Magic Door, No. 88-CV-1396 (1992).

13. Hensley v. Harford Memorial Hospital, No. 83-526120. (1992). Medical Malpractice Verdicts, Settlements & Experts, 8 (3), 22.

14. Beltran v. Downey Community Hospital (1992). Medical Malpractice Verdicts, Settlements & Experts, 8 (5), 30.

Chapter 8

Assuming Others Are Responsible for Your Duties

The theory that the surgeon is legally accountable for everything that goes wrong in the operating room is no longer accepted. For example, with the development of principles of individual accountability and professional liability, it was clear that anesthesia should bear its own legal responsibility. In recognition of this fact, separate anesthesia consent forms are now used in most states. This same concept has also extended liability principles to the nurse in the operating room: each individual in this room is accountable for his or her own actions. It is therefore imperative that nurses know what their responsibilities are and do not assume that others will do their job.

SPONGE AND INSTRUMENT COUNTS

Nowhere is this development in case law more apparent than in the cases involving sponge and instrument counts. In the original cases involving this issue, the surgeon was held responsible if a foreign object was retained in the patient. As the cases evolved, this came to be a shared responsibility for both the surgeon and the nurses involved in counts. In more recent cases, the nurses and/or hospital on behalf of the nurses has been held solely accountable for this issue.

In *Robinson v. N.E. Alabama Regional Medical Center*,[1] the patient had a vaginal hysterectomy and during the next 5 months visited her doctor five times complaining of pain, nausea, vomiting, inability to sleep, and dizziness. In a pelvic sonogram, a mass suspected of being an ovarian cyst was identified as a sponge. The surgeon indicated that the circulating nurse had told him the sponge count was correct. However, one of the vaginal packs had been cut in half. The jury awarded $250,000. The court held that the surgeon had the right to rely upon the sponge count of the nurses. In *Krieger v. Humana Hospital Biscayne*,[2] a laparotomy pad was left in a patient. She then needed 18 inches of her bowel resected and had continuing diarrhea and pain. The case was settled for $134,500 before trial.

Some of these cases are clearly indefensible, and the hospital settles rather than attempts to defend. If witnesses are not credible or if a policy is not followed without a documented reason in the patient's chart, the case may be difficult to defend and may be settled. An additional reason for settlement occurs when health care providers engage in **jousting**, or blaming one another. This behavior must be avoided at all costs since it only serves to make the plaintiff's case much easier to prove. Nurses and physicians must avoid accusing each other when the patient has an adverse outcome but no one has actually been negligent.

In all malpractice cases, it is important to determine the standard of care used *at the time of the incident*. In *Hillman v. California Hospital Medical Center*,[3] the plaintiff had a caesarean section and appendectomy and hysterectomy, and subsequently underwent exploratory laparotomy for bleeding. Approximately 20 years later, after developing a urinary infection, she underwent an x-ray study which revealed the presence of a 7-inch pair of surgical scissors in her abdomen. The defense successfully argued that no standard of practice existed at the time of the initial surgery regarding the counting of surgical instruments. Since the standard of care is applied at the time of the care of the patient rather than when the case is initiated, it is vital to retain policies and procedures that can be used in proof.

In many states, like Pennsylvania, a **discovery statute** exists which states that the statute of limitations does not begin to run until the patient discovers the harm suffered. The patient then has 2 years to begin his or her lawsuit. This has led to a whole series of cases known as the "Kelly in the Belly" series because patients did not know of the retained foreign object until some future date.

POSITIONING AND OPERATIVE SITE

Since operations are largely a team endeavor, identifying the accountable individual for an injury in the operating room can be a very difficult task. One of the most common problems is the patient who develops a neurological deficit after surgery. Sometimes this is the result of improper positioning, but who is actually responsible for the positioning of a specific patient may be impossible to determine. It is generally agreed that anesthesia is responsible for the original positioning of the patient; however, sometimes the surgeon enters and requests that the position of the patient be altered. Since other staff, including nurses, are usually responsible for carrying out the positioning direction, liability may be shared for their own physical activity.

"Doctor operates on wrong side; removes patient's only kidney."[4] Unfortunately, headlines like this do appear in the literature. The performance of surgery on the wrong side, for the wrong limb or wrong eye, or even on the wrong patient is a much too frequent occurrence and a risk manager's nightmare. Therefore the importance and necessity of preoperative patient identification, procedure verification, and confirmation of the correct operative site cannot be stressed enough.

One system worth considering has been developed by Dr. Robert Brittain, a thoracic surgeon and well-known risk management consultant. With this system, the surgeon requires that both the circulating nurse and the anesthesiologist ensure that the following five items are on the patient's chart at the time of surgery or the case will be canceled: (1) an admission note by the nurse indicating the correct side; (2) an admission note by a physician indicating the correct side; (3) x-rays (if any) showing the correct side; (4) the operative permit showing the correct side; and (5) a note in the chart stating that either the circulating nurse or the anesthesiologist asked the patient to identify the correct side. Again, all five items must be present and must consistently show the same side before surgery can begin.

In *Haye v. Nygaard and Porter Memorial Hospital,*[5] the plaintiff, age 30, alleged that the orthopedic surgeon had performed surgery on the right knee when it was supposed to be performed on the left knee. He claimed he was no longer able to participate in sports and recreational activities following the surgery. The doctor maintained that a nurse at the hospital prepped the wrong knee. He also argued that the right knee had problems not yet recognized and the patient actually benefited from the surgery. The jury returned a $25,000 verdict against the doctor.

BURNS

More traditional liability cases in the operating room are those involving burns to patients. In one case, failure to ground a bovie pad properly during rhinoplasty caused burns requiring grafting and 20 days of hospitalization. The jury awarded $117,440.[6] In *Harper v. Sparrow Hospital,*[7] the orthopedic patient alleged negligence in applying the bovie pad but defendants contended that the size and location of the irritation was not consistent with an electrical burn and that the patient was sensitive to prep solutions and suffered an idiosyncratic reaction. The jury returned a verdict for the defense. While this case does not illustrate an assumption about the responsibility of others, it does indicate another type of dangerous assumption.

HOW TO AVOID LIABILITY

Avoiding liability in these cases, as in many others, often involves being precise in one's descriptions of the event. Unfortunately, in some malpractice cases what the nurse has described as a "burn" actually is a pressure mark. There may be a huge difference in defending a "burn" case and a case involving a pressure area. This fact emphasizes the need for careful charting.

Comprehensive charting is also a necessity. In a recent unreported opinion. a patient slid off the operating room table while still awake. The nurse failed to document the event. When asked why, the nurse stated there was no space on the surgical record to document this unusual event. However, there is no law suggesting that the operative record need to be only one page, and an additional page can always be added. Unfortunately, such an omission may appear to be an attempt to misrepresent the care given the patient.

Sometimes the nurse in the operating room does not chart because he or she presumes that the surgeon will chart it. This is a dangerous assumption; the nurse has an independent legal responsibility to chart significant events. It is also another example of assuming someone else is responsible.

NOTES

1. Robinson v. N.E. Alabama Regional Medical Center, 548 So.2d 439 (Ala. 1989).

2. Krieger v. Humana Hospital Biscayne, No. 88-26042. (1989). *Medical Malpractice Verdicts, Settlements & Experts, 5* (11), 62.

3. Hillman v. California Hospital Medical Center. (1987). *Medical Malpractice Verdicts, Settlements & Experts, 3* (12), 24.

4. Brown, Judith, RN, J.D. (1992). Pennsylvania Medical Society Liability Insurance Company, *PRN Newsletter, 14* (5), 1.

5. Haye v. Nygaard and Porter Memorial Hospital. (1992). *Medical Malpractice Verdicts, Settlements & Experts, 8* (1), 43.

6. Siracusa v. Valley Park Medical Center. (1988). *Medical Malpractice Verdicts, Settlements & Experts, 4* (1), 32.

7. Harper v. Sparrow Hospital. (1992). *Medical Malpractice Verdicts, Settlements & Experts, 8* (4), 41.

Assuming Responsibility for Informed Consent

Another pitfall exists for the nurse who intrudes upon the physician's obligation to obtain the patient's informed consent. This intrusion may be the result of hospital policy, physician request, or the nurse's or hospital's misunderstanding of this particular issue. Hospitals sometimes do not seem to understand that a policy that allows nurses to participate in the informed consent procedure increases liability exposure for the hospital and the nurse.

DEFINITION OF INFORMED CONSENT

The heart of the informed consent law is the patient's right of self-determination. An adult who is competent has the right to make decisions about his or her own health care; in order to make those decisions, he or she needs sufficient information. Since the patient must be competent in order to provide an informed consent, it is important to define competence. For the purpose of medical decision making, this means the capacity to understand, at a given moment in time, the nature of the explanation that is being given as well as the ramifications of any decisions made. It is the physician's legal duty to determine the competency of the patient. Drugs or sedation may raise a presumption of incapacity, but that presumption may be refuted by an assessment of the patient.

Legally, this information includes a description of the nature of the procedure, the benefits of the procedure, alternatives to the procedure (including the consequences of having nothing done), and most importantly, the risks and complications of the procedure. Since the physician performing the procedure is in the best position to have the above knowledge as well as specific awareness of the individual patient's condition which may influence the possibility of complications, it is clearly the physician who should obtain the patient's consent to surgery.

Since most informed consent cases deal with elective procedures, it makes sense for the physician to actually obtain the patient's signature in the office when the patient reviews the initial explanation and actually decides whether he or she will have the surgery performed. The consent form may be valid as long as 6 months if neither the patient's condition nor the procedure and its risks change. Hospital policy should recognize this legal principle. The physician's office can then send the form to the hospital when the patient is actually admitted. This procedure also reinforces the legal concept that the form is simply a special kind of documentation; it is the discussion that is actually the "informed consent." *Informed consent is an educational process, it is not a form.*

THE COURT'S VIEWPOINT

This procedure is crucial because courts have generally held that the physician is responsible for informed consent. In a Missouri case, the court held that the patient's attending physician, not the hospital, was under a duty to obtain the patient's consent to a vein-stripping operation. The hospital had no obligation to find out whether the physician had, in fact, explained the risks and alternatives to surgery, especially where there was an executed consent form.[1]

In another case, a woman who was 9 months pregnant suffered direct trauma to her abdomen when she struck the steering wheel of her car during a collision. The patient's obstetrician examined her in a hospital emergency department, ordered fetal heart monitoring, and left the hospital. When the nurse who was monitoring the fetal heart tones informed the obstetrician by telephone that the test results were "equivocal" and that the patient continued to complain of abdominal numbness, she was told to send the patient home with instructions to return the following morning for additional monitoring. The patient and her husband were not informed of the equivocal test results. The next day, when tests indicated fetal distress, a caesarean section was performed and a permanently brain-damaged male infant was delivered. The couple sued, claiming that the hospital had a duty to inform the woman of the equivocal nature of the fetal monitoring results. The court held that the medical decision as to the test's significance was the physician's to determine, and that the hospital was not required to ensure that the patient's consent was fully informed.[2]

Physicians frequently question the usefulness and value of a signed consent form. However, the record shows that these forms are extremely important. Sometimes patients claim lack of informed consent even in the presence of a signed form, but juries seldom accept this argument. In *Graff v. Malawer*,[3] the patient, a 58-year-old male, was diagnosed as suffering from chondrosarcoma of the left pelvic area. The defendant testified that he told the plaintiff that he planned to perform a surgical procedure on the patient's left pelvis in order to save his leg, but also informed him of the possible hemipelvectomy and the patient signed a form. The plaintiff's brother testified that he and the plaintiff had discussed the possibility of amputation prior to surgery. The court held that the evidence overwhelmingly established that the plaintiff had given his informed consent to the possible necessity of an amputation.

In a Louisiana case, the court stated that the uniform consent form signed by the patient created a presumption that she had been advised of the risks connected with the proposed procedure and had given an informed consent. She had bilateral laminectomies performed and lost sphincter and bladder control.[4]

In another case, the court held that the signed consent form binds the patient if there is no significant misrepresentation. The patient, a licensed practical nurse, visited a physician with multiple problems traced to obesity, and the surgeon recommended a stapling procedure. Following surgery, the incision did not completely heal. The court held that the defendant did not induce consent by misrepresentation. It reasoned that the patient understood the procedure and realized that willpower was necessary to achieve weight loss results. Moreover, the signed consent form expressly rejected any guarantees as to treatment and a guaranteed weight loss.[5]

It is important that the consent form be used as a consistent vehicle for documentation to ensure that the physician does not omit some significant portion of his or her discussion with the patient.

THE NURSE'S ROLE

As already stated, when the physician obtains the patient's signature on the consent form, he or she is merely validating that the consent conversation with the patient has occurred. Since it is clearly the physician's responsibility to obtain the patient's consent, it follows that the physician's responsibility extends to the completion of the document. However, sometimes the nurses are asked to witness the document. If this is permitted under hospital policy, the nurse should actually witness the physician obtaining the patient's signature on the form.

In *Petriello v. Kalman*,[6] the patient sued her physician and the hospital for negligence and improper consent after her uterus ruptured and portions of her small intestine were lost due to excessive suction during a dilatation and curettage. Before the procedure, she had been given preoperative medication by the nurse, even though the consent form had not yet been signed. She was asked to sign the consent in the surgical holding area by the physician, and her signature was witnessed by an operating room nurse, who noted on the form that the patient was "alert and oriented." Hospital policy required signature prior to medication; however, although violation of work rules can be viewed as evidence of negligence, these rules do not of themselves establish standards of care. The important point is that the court held that the duty to obtain consent was solely the physician's responsibility. It stated that the delegation to the operating room supervisor of the responsibility for ensuring that the form had been signed could hardly have been intended to require her to fulfill the function of the attending physician in obtaining an actual informed consent, nor could these rules be deemed to have authorized the operating room nurse to countermand the judgment of the attending physician as to whether the patient had given an informed consent.

In *Ritter v. Delaney*,[7] the patient argued, fortunately unsuccessfully, that the hospital had become the agent of the operating surgeon because the physician wrote an order requiring the nurses to have the patient sign the form. The nurse had followed the order. The court stated that only the operating physician, not the hospital, must get a patient's consent to perform a surgical procedure, in this case, a carotid enterectomy.

If the nurse does suspect that consent is lacking or invalid for any reason, he or she should contact a nursing supervisor or the attending physician, and the physician should be asked to speak with the patient. The nurse should not attempt to carry out the consent discussion on behalf of the physician, for the nurse may become jointly liable for negligent nondisclosure along with the physician. Once the physician has been clearly advised of the problem with the consent, it becomes the physician's responsibility to decide how to rectify the situation.[8]

NOTES

1. Ackerman v. Lerwick, 676 S.W.2d 318 (Mo. 1985).

2. Alexander v. Gonser, 711 P.2d 347 (Wash. 1985).

3. Graff v. Malawer. (1991). *Medical Malpractice Verdicts, Settlements & Experts,* 7 (9), 31.

4. Hondroulis v. Schuhmacher, 531 So.2d 450 (La. 1988).

5. Rozlovsky, Fay. Consent to Treatment: A Practical Guide, 2d ed. (1990) Little, Brown and Co. P.92.

6. Petriello v. Kalman, 576 A.2d 474 (Conn. 1990).

7. Ritter v. Delaney, 790 W.S.2d 29 (Tex. 1990).

8. Horty, Springer, (1991). The form versus the consent. *Patient Care Law,* Action Kit for Hospital Law. (Pa. January 1991).

Chapter 10

Wrongfully Disclosing Confidential Information

The wrongful disclosure of confidential information is actionable and is a pitfall. The determination of what is wrongful disclosure and what is appropriate disclosure is based largely upon the facts of a particular situation. However, some issues fall more clearly into one category or the other.

DISCLOSURE OF MEDICAL RECORDS

The wrongful disclosure of medical records is an obvious pitfall and also rather easy to avoid. All requests for the release of a patient's medical chart after discharge should be referred to the medical records department. The hospital will have a detailed policy and procedure that is consistently followed and is effective against the wrongful disclosure of information.

In general, this policy will require that the appropriate person gives the appropriate authorization. This individual is usually the patient, but if the patient is incompetent or no longer alive, the right right to review the medical record will be transferred either by state law or common law. In most jurisdictions, the right to authorize release of a record passes to the next of kin as defined by law. The next of kin in most jurisdictions is first of all the spouse, then adult children, then parents if living, and finally siblings. This means that adult children have rights only if the spouse is no longer alive. (These rules are generally followed in consent and refusal of treatment cases as well.)

The appropriate authorization designed by the medical records department in conjunction with risk management or legal services will indicate that, depending on what information is contained in the patient's chart, differing releases may be necessary. For instance, if drug or alcohol treatment information or a psychiatric diagnosis or treatment is included, the patient should be told specifically what information is stated in the record. Sometimes patients will refute the accuracy of such information, and they should have the opportunity to do so before their chart is released. For example, the patient's medical history may suggest that the patient stated he drank a case of beer each day; the patient's version may be that he said he drank a case of beer each week. Regardless of whose version is correct, the patient should have the opportunity to add a letter to the chart explaining his or her version. *Under no circumstances should material ever be removed or deleted from the patient's chart.*

Testing for the presence of the HIV virus is another example of sensitive chart information that may require special consent under state law prior to release. The inclusion of this information in the patient's chart is extremely important; the material should be included just like any other clinically significant information that may be material to the case of the patient. When the AIDS virus was first identified, some hospitals ran into a pitfall by removing this information from the patient's medical record because of its sensitivity. It is important to remember that *all* information on the patient's medical record is both confidential and sensitive.

Allowing patients access to their medical records while they are in the hospital is another issue that should be directed by policy and procedure so that actions by all personnel are consistent. In most states, with the advent of the patients' rights movement, patients do have a right to access the contents of their medical record, even though technically the hospital may be the owner of the paper itself. An appropriate procedure would include obtaining the patient's signature on the appropriate authorization and making sure a third party is present while the patient reviews the chart. The presence of a third party, preferably a clinical person such as the patient's representative, will give the patient an opportunity to clarify any information he or she may not understand or that may be illegible on the record. This will also ensure that the patient does not alter or remove any information from the chart.

In this connection, it is particularly important to realize that patients who are requesting access to their chart are frequently expressing a *cry for help.* These are often patients who do not feel they are getting sufficient information about their own care. Since this feeling may result from a failure of communication between the physician and the patient, the attending physician should always be notified of the patient's request for his or her chart. This gives the physician an opportunity to talk to the patient. In some states, the physician is permitted to deny the patient access to his or her chart if the physician will document that information in the chart may be deleterious to the patient. In that event, the right to review the record may still pass to the next of kin. For example, the physician who charted "patient's blood pressure elevated due to extramarital affair," had great difficulty when the patient requested to read his chart. Needless to say, physicians need to be cautious about their judgments and expressions on a patient's chart.

DISCLOSURE OF OTHER INFORMATION

Other kinds of patient information can also be wrongfully disclosed. In Midland, Texas, for example, a respiratory therapist was fired for photographing Jessica McClure shortly after her celebrated rescue from an abandoned well in 1987. The *New York Times* purchased the photographs taken by the therapist, and he was later fired for violating hospital policies concerning release of patient information. He claimed he had the mother's permission to photograph, but a state district court dismissed his suit.[1]

Many cases deal with the wrongful disclosure of oral information. This may be the patient's diagnosis or perhaps even the fact that the patient is in the hospital. It is important to remember that patients do not become public figures simply because they are in the hospital. Patients with cancer, cosmetic surgery, or AIDS may not want to share their diagnosis with others.

Hospitalization alone may be a nondisclosure issue for many patients, and those who are receiving treatment for any reason have the expectation of privacy.

Recognizing this, nurses should operate under a *need to know* standard. If they are involved in the care of the patient, then they should be given the appropriate information; however, if not involved in the care, then the information should not be shared, perhaps except for educational or research purposes, and then with the identity of the patient protected insofar as possible.

This means, among other things, that information about patients should not be casually discussed in elevators and cafeterias. Hospital staff should be cautioned about these issues, and in fact, disclosure of confidential information should be a basis for disciplinary action. Going home and talking about patients to friends and family may also result in a basis for legal action. Health care providers should realize that because they work in the health care delivery system, *they are privileged to become aware of a great deal of information about people that is clearly of a private nature.* New employees and all students should be oriented to this issue.

This lesson is somewhat hard to learn because many behaviors that are actually an invasion of privacy or a breach of confidentiality have been casual practices in health care for some time. For example, posting the operating room schedule in a public area where anyone can read who is having what surgery performed is technically an invasion of the right to privacy.[2]

In smaller hospitals, the publication of admissions and discharges in the local newspaper or over the local radio station *without patient consent* is another example of a violation. The once common practice of publishing birth announcements in the local newspaper without parental consent is yet another example. These are not deliberate violations, but rather practices that have arisen through simple lack of consideration.

As patients have become more aware of their rights and as the rights to privacy and confidentiality have continued to evolve in society, more and more of these principles have been applied to health care. In one hospital, the risk manager received a call from an angry young man complaining that the birth announcement in the morning paper identified him as the father of a new baby. He was not; the mother had lied, and he himself was about to enter the seminary. The hospital apologized and changed its procedure; now both father and mother provide written authorization.

Obviously, the public relations staff must be careful when using patient information. A California hospital published a brochure using the patient's name, photograph, and medical records. The jury awarded $274,000 for emotional distress.[2]

Although the previous examples deal with the issue of privacy, the *legal* action of invasion of privacy usually deals with a physical action as opposed to the spoken work. In *Verneuil v. Poirier*, a former hospital employee brought a defamation action against the hospital and an **invasion of privacy action** against her supervisor, whom she alleged had lifted her sheet and gown to view her surgical incision after she underwent surgery at the hospital. She had been employed as a cardiology technician and was admitted to have her ovary removed. She complained about her supervisor's actions and was fired. The appeals court held that the finding of invasion of privacy was supported by testimony of the patient that she saw the hospital employee lift up her gown and sheet to view her incision even though she was still under the effects of anesthesia, and by testimony that the hospital employee had asked questions concerning her incision and wound that firmly suggested that he had viewed the patient's body. However, the court held that the award of $75,000 was excessive and reduced it to $15,000.[3]

This example also shows that a special problem exists when a hospital employee becomes a patient. To ensure the privacy of employees, especially high-profile, well-known individuals, the hospital may allow an alias to be used when the individual undergoes treatment.

NOTES

1. Author not listed (1990). Texas court dismisses suit by fired hospital employee. *Modern Healthcare, 20* (21), 20.

2. Banks v. Charter Hospital of Long Beach, SOC-99996. (1992). *Medical Malpractice Verdicts, Settlements & Experts, 8* (10), 19.

3. Verneuil v. Poirier, 589 So.2d 1205 (La. 1991).

Chapter 11

Making Reckless Accusations

Tension runs high in hospitals. Nurses, physicians, and other hospital employees are constantly working under stress, and tempers can flare. So, it is not unexpected that personality conflicts arise from time to time; the difficulty is sometimes determining what is a personality conflict and what is a matter for litigation.[1] This chapter discusses two types of allegations—constructive discharge and defamation.

CONSTRUCTIVE DISCHARGE

Sometimes working conditions may seem so impossible that an employee feels compelled to resign. In such a situation, a nurse may make the allegation of **constructive discharge**: although technically he or she resigns, the nurse argues that this amounts to a discharge because of the intolerable circumstances. Such an allegation, however, must be based on something other than subjective opinion. The nurse must also prove that the employer violated public policy in some way. In *Seery v. Yale—New Haven Hospital*,[2] a nurse anesthetist and an anesthesiologist sued the hospital for wrongful discharge, alleging that the hospital forced them to work with an impaired physician and that the hospital violated public policy by failing to report the physician to the Connecticut Department of Health Services. Diane Seery, a nurse anesthetist, and Thomas Guckian, a staff anesthesiologist, had been employed at the Yale–New Haven Hospital from 1971 to 1981. In 1979, both were assigned to the hospital's one-day surgery unit. The court recounted the facts precipitating the problem:

In July, 1981, a second anesthesiologist, E-Fun Tsai, was assigned to the one-day surgery unit to help with the increased number of patients. Tsai was returning to the hospital after a six-month leave of absence. Tsai and the hospital had agreed to the leave of absence following a January, 1981 incident in which Tsai had needed assistance in adminis- tering anesthesia because, as she admitted, on that day she had ingested two prescription sedatives. This incident followed reported episodes in October, 1977, and October 1980, in which Tsai admitted that her ingestion of prescription sedatives had interfered with her duties. The hospital was aware of these incidents, but did not notify the State Department of Health during her six-month leave of absence, the hospital insisted that Tsai seek psychiatric treatment, which she did. A report filed by her psychiatrist recommended that she be placed on daytime clinical duties. Pursuant to this report, Tsai was assigned to the one-day surgery unit on the condition that she continue psychiatric treatment. The assignment was also conditioned on the approval of Guckian, who was told to monitor Tsai.

On November 9, 1981, Nurse Seery claimed that she was subjected to an unprovoked physical and verbal attack by Tsai. Tsai claimed that Seery was the aggressor. There were no witnesses to this incident. November 12, both Seery and Tsai received letters reprimanding them equally for unprofessional conduct and warning them that any repetition would result in "severe disciplinary action up to and including discharge." These letters were placed in their respective personnel files.

Seery strenuously protested and, after speaking with the chief of staff, she obtained a meeting with the chief of anesthesiology and other hospital administrators, and demanded that the letter be removed. The hospital refused to remove the letter, and, thereafter, Seery pursued the hospital's grievance procedure and obtained legal counsel. Her lawyer wrote a letter demanding that the letter be removed and adding that if her demands were not met she would "go public". On or about November 13, Seery called the Professional Standard Review Organization (PSRO), which is a federal organization that monitors the quality of care given to Medicare patients, to complain that there was a doctor at Yale–New Haven Hospital who might be impaired . . . .

In February, 1982, Seery pursued the hospital's three-step grievance procedure. At the first meeting, Seery stated that she was there to rescue her reputation and that she wanted the written warning removed from her file and a written apology from Tsai. At the meeting, Tsai made an oral apology and it was agreed to remove the warning from the file in three months. Seery stated that she did not accept this offer because she refused to accept any blame for the incident and she wanted a written apology from Tsai.

Seery then pursued the second step of the grievance process and put the grievance in writing and sent it to the vice president of the department. Seery received a written response stating that he found the warning letter to be appropriate and that it would be inappropriate to force Tsai to reiterate her apology in writing.

Seery still was not satisfied. At the third step, Seery met with the hospital's executive vice president. Guckian attended this meeting as Seery's advisor. At this meeting, both Guckian and Seery attacked the credibility of Tsai's version of the altercation by referring to her history of personal problems. In addition, Guckian recounted two recent cases in which he questioned Tsai's medical judgment. Under questioning, Guckian admitted that he had neither investigated nor taken corrective action with respect to these two cases even though he was the anesthesiologist in charge of the unit. An investigation on behalf of the hospital was then initiated

The hospital also denied Seery's request for a leave of absence from March 1 to March 5. The hospital claimed it denied Seery's request because Guckian had already been scheduled to be away for the same period and the hospital did not want to be shorthanded. Seery was absent despite the denial of her request. She had sought the leave for two reasons: because she desired treatment for a medical problem, and because Tsai would be left in charge of the unit while Guckian was away. When Seery returned, she received another letter of reprimand. She testified that she felt that the hospital was paving the way for her dismissal. A few days later, on March 29, she learned that Guckian would be going on an extended leave of absence. Because she felt that she would be left under the direction of Tsai, Seery immediately resigned. Seery testified that she felt the conditions would be intolerable because Tsai was not in control of herself and was not in a condition to control the unit. . . .

. . . [On] April 2, the hospital had concluded that there was no basis for any concern about either Tsai or the two incidents reported by Guckian. About this time, the chief of anesthesiology wrote a memorandum that was supportive to Tsai. On April 29, the chief of staff, in response to this memorandum, wrote a letter in which he stated "I wonder if it isn't Dr. Guckian we should think about terminating." [Seery and Guckian] contend that they put forth sufficient evidence for a jury to decide reasonably and legally that they had been discharged in violation of public policy. . . .

Seery's complaint alleged that she had been "constructively discharged" in violation of public policy. The hospital maintained that it did not discharge Seery, but rather that she voluntarily resigned.

Constructive discharge occurs when an employer renders an employee's working conditions so difficult and intolerable that a reasonable person would feel forced to resign. A claim of constructive discharge must be supported by more than the employee's subjective opinion that the job conditions have become so intolerable that he or she was forced to resign.

Normally, an employee who resigns is not regarded as having been discharged, and thus would have no right of action for abusive discharge. Through the use of [the term] constructive discharge, the law recognizes that an employee's "voluntary" resignation may be, in reality, a dismissal by the employer. . . . [However]. . . the employee must still prove that the dismissal, in whatever form, occurred for a reason violating public policy.

The trial court found Seery and Guckian failed to provide any evidence that Tsai was impaired when they worked with her and ruled in favor of the hospital.

The appeals court agreed and stated:

. . . "[Seery and Guckian] failed to produce any evidence that Tsai's ability was impaired during the time she was employed in the one-day surgery unit." The [trial] court refused to consider as evidence any of the incidents that occurred before Tsai joined the one-day surgery department. The court found that the only evidence offered to support the allegation that Tsai was impaired was evidence of the Tsai-Seery fight, and evidence of the two incidents mentioned by Guckian. The two incidents were investigated by hospital staff and determined to be unrelated to any impairment due to drug use and Guckian conceded that they were matters of judgment. The dispute with Tsai was investigated by the chief of anesthesia after Guckian himself took no action; he found that the cause of this incident could not be determined.

The Appeals court stated: [In their complaint, Seery and Guckian] each alleged that "[they] became aware that one of the anesthesiologists employed in the one-day surgery department had a history of serious drug abuse and showed signs of volatile behavior consistent with the *continued* abuse. It became increasingly apparent to [them] that this drug problem had the potential to greatly hinder and *did in fact* hinder ability to perform duties as an anesthesiologist and it was becoming unsafe for said
doctor to continue performing said duties unless under the consistent scrutiny of other professionals on the staff. Hence, said doctor's presence in the department seriously undermined the effectiveness and efficiency of the department. . . ."

[Seery and Guckian] were bound by the allegation of their complaint to prove that Tsai was impaired during the time she worked with Seery on the one-day surgery unit. . . . Stripped of the earlier Tsai episodes, the evidence that remained before the jury consisted of only the two incidents mentioned by Guckian, and the fight. Guckian's testimony made it clear that he did not consider Tsai to be incompetent. Even if the jury might have accepted the claim that [Seery and Guckian] were [constructively] discharged, they could not reasonably and legally have concluded from this evidence that Tsai was impaired at the time of the discharges. We agree with the trial court that "because there was no credible evidence that the physician in question was impaired, during the time period pleaded, the [hospital was] not guilty of violating public policy.

This case clearly shows how careful nurses must be in their allegations. Because the court found no evidence of an active impairment *at the time under dispute*, the hospital could not be found to have violated public policy by failing to report the "impairment." Thus, even if Seery and Guckian were in fact "pressured out"—perhaps because of their own disruptive conduct—such an action could not be characterized as a "constructive discharge."

The previous case is presented in detail to illustrate the analysis of the court in determining these difficult issues. It is also important to remember that employees-at-will, such as nurses, may be discharged with little recourse. The term "at-will" refers to the employers legal right to terminate any employee at any time without reason and with-out the need for justification. Right or wrong, few of the perceived principles underlying such terminations—such as freedom of speech or professional autonomy—rise to the level of public policy concerns in the eyes of most courts.

This does not mean that nurses who suspect that a physician is impaired should hesitate to report unusual incidents, in accordance with hospital policy, to nurse or hospital management. Hospitals clearly have both a vital interest and a legal duty to respond to such concerns with timely and thorough investigations. In other words, the Seery case should not be understood to imply that such reports by nurses (or other employees) are inappropriate, or that hospitals have no responsibility to investigate them and to act on their findings. (On the contrary, this hospital had already acted on earlier findings.)[3]

The Seery-Tsai case also shows how careful hospitals must be when dealing with drug and alcohol issues. Individuals recovering from drug or alcohol impairments are protected under the Federal Rehabilitation Act, and now under the Americans with Disabilities Act as well. Any employment actions with respect to these individuals must be supported by examples which document active impairment.[4]

In many situations, hospitals may terminate a nurse for inappropriate, negative comments that are not protected communication from the public policy standpoint. In Pennsylvania, a psychiatric nurse was discharged on the basis of unacceptable and inappropriate conduct which included negative comments about the hospital and its staff and instructions to new employees to ignore violations of hospital policy. For example, she stated that one-half of administration should be fired and that new employees should "turn their heads" when confronted with patients engaged in sexual activities. This evidence directly contradicted the hospital's policy. Prior to her discharge, she had been counseled for her negative comments and attitude. In court, she argued that her misconduct, according to the personnel manual, fell under unsatisfactory performance which required a lesser form of reprimand. The court stated that the personnel manual was only a guideline and did not have the force and effect of law. The court found just cause for termination; her performance was considered impaired on the basis of her conduct with new employees, her advice to ignore violations of hospital policy, and her negative comments about the hospital and its staff.[5]

DEFAMATION

One allegation that is frequently made by hospital employees is **defamation**, which generally is defined as any communication that tends to harm a person's reputation, lowers him or her in the estimation of the community, or deters other people from associating or dealing with him or her.[6] Defamation may be either written, known as libel, or oral, known as slander. This sort of charge is usually made against the hospital by employees who have been fired. From 1983 to 1988, over 8,000 defamation suits were filed by employees against their former employer.[7] This may explain the tendency of employers during that time period, when responding to reference requests about former employees, to supply the bare minimum of information: "name, rank, and serial number."

THE RIGHT TO INFORM

Although defamation suits are a real concern for management, employers are not defenseless, and they do have a recognized right to inform. For example, on an application for employment at a hospital, a nurse anesthetist had indicated that an inquiry could be made of her former employer, an anesthesia service where she had been given a notice of termination. When contacted, the former employer indicated that she lacked professional competence. When her hospital employment application was denied, she sued the anesthesia service for slander. The court found the former employer not liable on the basis that employers and prospective employers have a legitimate interest in employment-related information.[8]

Moreover, employers may get into more trouble if they *fail* to warn prospective employers adequately about dangerous or unfit employees.[9] In one case, for example, a Boston hospital sued another institution for failing to inform the employer that a physician the latter had hired had been charged with rape.[10]

The Need for Caution

Truth is a complete defense to defamation charges. However, employers should still be cautious in their communications. Information regarding employee conduct or job performance should be limited to factual observations and should avoid conclusions that are drawn from those facts. For example, consider the following hypothetical situation. A hospital's director of nursing services notices that a registered nurse smells of alcohol and has slurred speech. The employee admits to the nursing director that she had three drinks at lunch with friends before she came to work at 3:00 p.m. Because this was the third occurrence within 9 months, the director fires the employee for "reporting to work in an impaired condition and alcoholism." Although the employee's termination may have been appropriate under the circumstances, the reason for termination given by the director could be defamatory.

First, except for slurred speech, there is no evidence that the nurse was impaired. The evidence only demonstrates that she had three drinks before she came to work and that she smelled of alcohol. Second, there is no evidence to establish that the nurse is an alcoholic. Because this was the third occurrence, it is distinctly possible that the nurse suffers from alcoholism, but there is scant *support* for this conclusion. A factual summary of the nurse's conduct and condition as the reason for discharge would have been preferable: "[While] on duty, nurse noticeably smelled alcohol, and speech was slurred. Nurse admitted having three drinks prior to reporting to work. This is the third time within nine months the employee has smelled of alcohol while at work."[11]

When giving references, employers can avoid pitfalls by developing a policy and sticking to it. Consider the "golden rule"—if you would like to know, then tell others. Discourage informal telephone inquiries, which can lead to misquotation of responses. Responses should always be in writing; this will also eliminate bogus calls from friends or relatives who are "testing the water" or hoping to trap an unwary employer into saying something that can be used as a basis for a defamation suit.

Finally, an individual should not be described a good employee if that is not true. If the employee was terminated for cause, this evidence would be used against the employer if the employee sues for wrongful discharge.[12] If the health care facility is cautious and honest in its references, the case will be defensible.

In *Pollock v. Baxter Manor Nursing Home,*[13] a food service specialist in a nursing home was discharged for clocking her daughters, also employees, in and out of work. Her termination interview and termination interview form gave good marks for work quality and productivity but unsatisfactory marks for "loyalty and honesty" and included the reason for her discharge. Her new prospective employer was provided a copy of the form after she had consented to release of all information regarding her previous employment. The court stated that the terminated employee is protected only from the release of false information.[14]

Protected and Unprotected Information

Courts have recognized that an efficient and effective business operation requires direct and unedited discussion regarding employees. Therefore, most employers' communications have a **qualified privilege**; that is some protection against a defamation claim. In order to receive this protection, the employer must have acted in good faith to protect a legitimate (business) interest, the statement must have been limited in scope and purpose, and publication must have been made only to appropriate parties in the proper manner. For example, in one case a hospital accounting supervisor's remarks to a hospital auditor concerning a former employee's alleged financial improprieties were protected by a qualified privilege from defamation claims by the former employee. The supervisor had reported to the auditor that the employee had made personal purchases of supplies on the hospital account and that she had food prepared in the hospital dietary department for personal social functions at her home. The court ruled that the auditor had a duty to investigate the finances of the hospital and the supervisor had a duty to furnish information, and that there was no evidence of malice or ill will.[15]

Some communications are protected by an **absolute privilege**: they cannot be used at all to support defamation allegations. In one instance, a registered nurse (RN) at a Veterans Administration hospital sued a licensed practical nurse (LPN) for both libel and slander. The RN had interpreted a medication order as morphine and had told the LPN to administer it to the patient. The LPN refused to give the medication because she did not think that the order was for morphine. The RN checked with the pharmacy and the doctor and discovered that the order was for magnesium sulfate. She contended that she then told the LPN to administer the right medication. The LPN contended that she had been ordered to give the wrong medication by the RN. The LPN discussed the correctness of the RN's interpretation of the order with another nurse, and the next day the head nurse directed the LPN to make a written report of the incident. The court held that the written report could not be the basis of a libel suit because reports made by federal officials (such as Veterans Administration nurses) in the course of disciplinary or other proceedings in which the official is acting under a duty to complete a report are protected by an absolute privilege. However, on the basis of the *oral* statements, the court refused to dismiss the action for slander. It found that there was a factual dispute as to what the LPN actually said to her colleague and that it was possible to conclude that the comments did impugn the plaintiff's professional competence. Since there was more than one plausible interpretation of the comments, the action was allowed to go to trial.[16]

In Minnesota, a jury awarded a nurse $50,000 in compensatory damages and $100,000 in punitive damages. The nurse had been assigned to work in the hospital's intensive care unit from a temporary nursing agency. During this assignment, the nurse cared for a terminally ill 98-year-old patient. This patient died from congestive heart failure the day after the nurse administered some pain medication following physician's orders. After the patient's death, the hospital contacted the nursing agency and stated that it would no longer accept the nurse's services. Two nurses employed in the intensive care unit drafted a memo to the hospital stating there had been no need for the nurse to give morphine to the patient and alleging that the nurse had used the narcotic in an attempt to hasten the patient's death. The memo also accused the nurse of being "sloppy and incomplete" in previous assignments. The nurse succeeded in suing both the hospital and nurses who drafted the memo for defamation.[17]

Finally, oral accusations may be used as evidence of defamation. In one case, a nurse was dismissed for unprofessional conduct because she had been openly critical of the physician's treatment of a postoperative patient. The charges she brought against the physician were dismissed by the hospital's grievance committee, and she was later reemployed by the hospital on the condition that she would not discuss hospital business outside the hospital. The physician, on learning of her reemployment, called the administrator and said, "I wanted to ask you if you would stoop so low as to hire that creep, that malignant son of a bitch, back to work for you in the hospital." He also stated that "she was unfit to care for patients. . . he could prove it. . . that he intended to make an issue of it." The nurse sued the physician for defamation and was awarded $17,500 in a jury verdict that was later reduced to $5,000 by the court, which claimed that provocation, although not an excuse for slander, was a mitigating factor in assessing punitive damages.[18]

The Defamation Quandary

"Do the sick do no harm," Florence Nightingale enjoined over a century ago. That classic duty would seem the very least nurses could do to honor their profession. Ironically, the very growth of nursing clinical capacities and technical responsibilities has multiplied nurses' opportunities for not only doing effective good but also for doing destructive harm. At the same time, the threat of a defamation suit can prevent us from carefully noting possible harm. How well are we guarding against exposure to hazards of incompetent or unethical nursing? Are we assuring the public, as we are professionally bound to do, that we are sufficiently monitoring and evaluating nursing care delivery? Public response at times suggest that we are not. A family member of one victim on a TV program kept asking, "Why didn't anyone check?" Health care workers and hospitals are faced with these questions: Why do we make it so easy to slip through the system? Is the life of a patient worth the cost of litigation?

In a recent article, a nurse discusses speaking to recruiters who indicate that a state board may not reveal actions and infractions against a nurse's license unless the inquiring institution specifically requests such information. Moreover, sanctions or restrictions from previous years may not be disclosed. Restrictions like these make it difficult for employers to give important information.[19]

Most managers are trying to hire the best person for the job. If they must rely primarily on instinct and a 1-hour interview, the possibility of hiring an unsuitable person is great. Many argue that this problem exists in any job, but incompetence in a computer programmer, for example, does not cause death or permanent injury, whereas health care practitioners hold patients' lives in their hands. Entrusting their lives to us, the public expects practitioners to do their utmost to safeguard and protect them.

Legislation granting immunity to former employers might help to alleviate the situation. For the present, however, a simpler solution is, once again, documentation. Proper documentation can convincingly substantiate unfavorable references to a grievance board or a court of law. It is true that busy nurse managers, forced into dual roles of clinical support and management, find that investigating and documenting problems is painful and time consuming. Often staff nurses shy away from revealing specific information about incidents, just as physicians tend to protect fellow physicians in compromising situations. However, as professionals, nurses are all obliged to come forward with information which points to incompetence or unethical, criminal practice among practitioners of nursing.

As part of the solution, senior administrators must foster an environment conducive to exposing such behaviors and to seeking disciplinary action. While avoiding witch-hunting, they should thoroughly investigate all complaints and ascertain and document the degree of credibility in the complaints. In addition, institutions must take necessary disciplinary actions which send messages to individuals, professional circles, and their communities that aberrant behavior will not be tolerated. One of the most crucial of those messages is that complete and accurate reference information, with sufficient documentation to establish its credit, will always be exchanged with those who hire nurses.[20]

As a final note, it must be said that administrators can also prevent unnecessary litigation by establishing a positive atmosphere. The hospital is a stressful environment for patients and for health care professionals. It is understandable that in this complex and fast-paced world tempers and temperaments will at times erupt in a manner that leads to actions for defamation. Exactly how often his occurs is difficult to identify because libel and slander are especially suitable for a negotiated settlement: at a later time, in a calmer setting, the patient or the nurse or doctor who was allegedly defamed may be willing to settle for an apology and reasonable compensation. Recognizing all of this, the nurse manager should create and foster an environment of mutual respect and consideration for the contributions and competencies of all types of health care professionals.

NOTES

1. Horty, John, Editor, (1991, August/September). I've Gotta Get Out of This Place. *Patient Care Law*, An Action-Kit Publication.

2. 554 A.2d 757 (Conn. Ct. App. 1989).

3. Horty, John, Editor, (1991, August/September). I've Gotta Get Out of This Place. *Patient Care Law*, An Action-Kit Publication.

4. Horty, John, Editor, (1991, August/September). I've Gotta Get Out of This Place. *Patient Care Law*, An Action-Kit Publication.

5. Kachmar v. Pennsylvania, 559 A.2d 606 (Pa. Commw. 1989)

6. Martin v. Lincoln General Hospital, 588 So.2d 1329 (La. App. 1991).

7. Stickler, K. Bruce and Nelson, Mark D. (1988). Defamation in the Workplace; Employer Rights, Risks, and Responsibilities. *Journal of Health and Hospital Law, 21* (5), 97.

8. Copithorne v. Framingham Union Hospital, 401 Mass. 860 (1988). (1989). *Medical Malpractice Verdicts, Settlements & Experts, 5* (3), 24.

9. Restatement (Second) of Torts ss559 (1977).

10. Stickler, K. Bruce and Nelson, Mark D. (1988). Defamation in the Workplace: Employer Rights, Risks, and Responsibilities. *Journal of Health and Hospital Law, 21* (5) 99.

11. Malone v. Longo, 463 F. Supp. 139 (D.D.N.Y. 1979).

12. Murray v. HealthEast. No. CV-90-1472 Dist. Minn. (March 7, 1991).

13. Farrell v. Kramer, 193 A.2d 560 (Maine 1963).

14. Gengler v. Phelps, 589 P.2d 1056 (N.M. Ct. of App. 1978); cert. denied, 558 P.2d 554 (N.M. Sup. Ct. 1979).

15. Trudeau, Stephanie E. (1992). Responding to Requests for References Requires Balancing Moral, Social and Legal Duties. *Hospital Law Newsletter, 9* (7), 1–3.

16. 536 F. Supp. 673 (U.S. D.C. W.D. Arkansas 1982).

17. Horty, John F. (1983, January) Truths a Strong Weapon in Firing Worker. *Modern Healthcare*, 136.

18. Farrell v. Kramer, 193 A 2d 560 (Me. 1963).

19. Turner, Barbara. (1992). Reputation: Can We Prevent the Harm? *Nursing Management, 23* (3), 54-60

20. Cournoyer, Carmelle Pellerin (1989). The Nurse Manager and the Law. (Rockville, M.D.: Aspen Publishers, Inc.).

Chapter 12

Failing to Act Like a Professional

Nurses are professionals who are personally accountable for their actions. This may include monitoring the care given to patients by physicians as well as nurses.

THE DUTY TO REPORT

In *Catron v. The Poor Sisters of St. Francis*, the court held that the hospital will be held liable if the nurse fails to report medical orders or care which could jeopardize the patient and the patient is harmed. In this case, the patient was hospitalized for an unintentional drug overdose. While in the hospital, an endotracheal tube was left in place for 5 days on physician's orders. When the tube was finally removed, the patient had difficulty breathing. A tracheostomy was performed, and at trial the patient could not speak above a whisper. The jury awarded $150,000 against the hospital. The hospital on appeal stated that the removal of this tube was a medical judgment. The court agreed that the hospital is usually not liable when the nurse follows orders given by the physician but that an exception exists when the nurse knows that the practice is not in accord with usual procedure. The court stated that the nurses should have reported the deviation to their supervisor.[1]

Guidelines for nursing staff often suggest that medical orders by physicians are to be questioned only if they are incomplete and inconsistent with accepted standards of practice or if there is sound basis for believing that carrying out the orders would cause severe and irreversible harm to the patient.[2] The extreme caution in such statements should not blind nurses to the fact that it is still legally their *duty* to report deviations. Moreover, in court the nurse may not be protected merely by relying on the physician's assertion that he or she will take full responsibility.

To avoid this pitfall, the hospital should establish a policy for nurses to follow when care provided to any patient is jeopardized. Nurses should state their concerns directly to the physician and inform the head nurse or the physician's supervisor (everyone in the hospital has a supervisor even though he or she may not know it!). The person who is notified then has the responsibility for following through and resolving the problem.

The duty to report questionable care includes not only the questions of competence or inappropriate medical orders but also bizarre or disruptive behavior or conduct which may be a symptom of impairment. Any hospital policy should include steps for reporting impaired or disruptive physicians.

These steps are important because even when a nurse is unsure about an issue, as long as there is a legitimate question, patients must be protected. After the report has been made, it should not be discussed with other nurses unless it is necessary for the protection of the patient. For example, a nurse from the day shift should inform the nurse on the next shift that a problem has arisen in regard to a particular patient's care.[3]

REASONABLE PROFESSIONAL CONDUCT

Deciding when one needs to report something, however, often cannot be based on policy. The hard fact is that in many cases nurses must rely on their judgment, and they themselves are often judged against the standard of reasonable professional conduct, which is established in court by expert witnesses. In a court of law, a deviation from a *professional* standard will be shown by the introduction of expert testimony. This is a significant distinction between the ordinary negligence case (such as liability in an automobile accident) and the malpractice case. In every negligence or malpractice proceeding, the injured party or plaintiff must prove that the defendant did something that a reasonable person in the same or similar circumstance would not have done, or did not do something that a reasonable person would have done. In a malpractice proceeding, however, it must be proven that a professional has deviated from what a reasonable professional person would have done in the same or similar circumstances. Therefore, an expert is required to give this testimony.[4]

In *Leonard v. Providence Hospital*,[5] an 81-year-old patient fell out of bed and sustained a fractured hip while in the hospital. She sued the hospital and a staff nurse because the side rails of her bed were not in a raised position. There was no physician order to have the side rails raised, and the physician had written nothing about ambulation precautions. The patient did not submit expert testimony to support her claim of negligence by the nurse. The case was brought under the Alabama Medical Liability Act, which has been interpreted as requiring expert medical testimony to establish the standard of care. In this case, the court ruled that the absence of a physician's order necessitated expert testimony to determine proper nursing practice.

In some situations this standard may help the nurse's case. In *Dixon v. Freuman*,[6] the physician ordered that the use of a Foley catheter be discontinued. The plaintiff alleged that the nurses should have kept the catheter in. The court held that in the absence of proof that the physician's order to discontinue the catheter was "clearly contraindicated by normal practice," the nurses and hospital could not be held liable for the occurrence of the fistula.

Obviously, it is not always easy to make such a determination. In *Bruce v. Memorial Mission Hospital, Inc.*,[7] the plaintiff, a 21-year-old man, came to the emergency room after swallowing between 50 and 120 Darvon tablets with three cans of beer. About 36 hours later, he had a heart attack and respiratory arrest and suffered severe brain damage. He alleged that nurses had not followed the doctor's instructions in treating him. The hospital contended that the orders were flexible and the nurses had followed them using their best judgment. The jury returned a verdict for the defendant. The plaintiff then asked the state supreme court to decide the narrow question of whether the trial judge should have given jurors more instructions pertaining to the nurse's duty to follow doctors' orders. The hospital opposed this, contending that the trial was about nursing judgment, not nursing obedience. The state supreme court split 3 to 3 on this issue.

THE DUTY TO DISOBEY IF NECESSARY

Unfortunately, professional conduct sometimes requires that nurses actually disobey physicians' orders. In one case, a 28-year-old woman was coming out of anesthesia in the operating room after routine surgery to remove an ovarian cyst. The anesthesiologist, operating room technician, operating surgeon, and circulating nurse were initially in the operating room with the patient. However, the operating surgeon left the room to prepare for another surgery and called for the circulating nurse to accompany him. The circulating nurse stated that she could not leave the room because she had not completed her postoperative monitoring. The physician persisted, and the nurse finally left the room with him. While the nurse was out of the room, the patient went into cardiac arrest. The anesthesiologist sent the operating room technician to obtain help and started cardiopulmonary resuscitation himself. However, he could not do this adequately without the aid of another person, and the patient was left completely paralyzed and in a permanent semicomatose state.

The patient's family brought suit against the hospital on the grounds that the nurse had abandoned the patient at a critical point in the postoperative stage. At trial, their attorney introduced the hospital's manual of procedure into evidence, which stated that the circulating nurse was a "member of the team who will be on hand to assist the anesthesiologist during the entire procedure." The nurse defended on the grounds that she was "being yelled at," but the jury ruled that the nurse and therefore the hospital were negligent and awarded the plaintiffs $982,000. The trial judge set aside the jury verdict and entered a judgment in favor of the hospital. On appeal, however, a higher court reversed the trial judge's decision and reinstated the jury's verdict. It found not only that the actions of the nurse constituted abandonment of the patient, but that this negligence was so obvious to a layperson that the plaintiffs did not need an expert witness to establish their case.[8] This is highly unusual.

Another case that involved following a physician's instructions was *Suburban Hospital v. Hadary*.[9] A patient was admitted to the hospital for a liver biopsy, a procedure that required insertion of a Menghini needle into the liver. These needles were kept in a cabinet in the minor surgery room. The upper two shelves in the cabinet were used for non-sterile needles and the bottom two for sterile needles. The shelves were not marked in any way. Prior to the biopsy, the physician who was to perform the procedure approached the nurse and stated,
"I want my needle." The nurse, who was assisting another physician engaged in minor surgery, replied, "Just a minute, I will get them for you." The physician responded, "No, no, I will get them." The nurse repeated what she had said, but the physician left the room quickly to obtain the needle himself. Not being familiar with the system of storing needles, he took an unsterilize needle from one of the top shelves instead of a sterilize needle from one of the bottom shelves. He then performed the biopsy with the unsterilize needle.

After the procedure, the nurse went to the cabinet and saw that the sterile needle that was supposed to have been used in the procedure was still in the cabinet. She informed the physician that he may have used an unsterilized needle. The physician asked the nurse not to discuss the incident with anyone, but he told the patient that he may have performed her biopsy with an unsterilized needle that had been used on a patient with liver disease. Because of this error, the patient was exposed to a risk of infectious hepatitis and had to undergo a series of massive injections that were very painful. In addition, while she was undergoing these injections she had to stop taking drug therapy for her psoriasis, which caused her condition to worsen. The patient later brought suit against both the physician and the hospital.

At trial, the nurse admitted that it was standard procedure for the nurse to obtain the needle for the physician. Both the physician and the hospital were held liable. As with the previous case, the court ruled that the negligence was so obvious to a layperson that the plaintiff did not need an expert witness to prove her case. The verdicts were confirmed on appeal.

HOW TO AVOID LIABILITY

These are obviously difficult situations, and some guidelines are needed for avoiding this pitfall. Nurses or any physician extenders can protect themselves and their institutions from liability in complying with a physician's order by doing the following:

- The nurse should be familiar with all pertinent hospital protocols and manuals.

- If a physician gives orders that violate these protocols or standard procedures, then the nurse must tell the physician what the protocols say or what the standard procedures are.

- If the physician insists that the nurse follow the order in question despite being informed of the procedures, a supervisor must be contacted and presented with the problem.

- In an emergency situation in which it is reasonably certain that following the physician's order will result in harm to the patient, the nurse has a legal duty to disobey the order and notify the supervisor.[10]

NOTES

1. Catron v. The Poor Sisters of St. Francis, 435 N.E.2d 305 (Ind. 1982).

2. Katz, Barbara F. (1983, April). Reporting and review of patient care: The nurse's responsibility. *Law, Medicine & Health Care*, 20.

3. Haddad, Linda. (1982). Nurses' Inaction Leads to Hospital Liability. *Patient Care Law, An Action-Kit Publication: Special Item, 4.*

4. Fiesta, Janine. (1988). *The law and liability: A guide for nurses* (2nd ed., pp. 46-47), New York: Wiley.

5. Leonard v. Providence Hospital, 590 So.2d 906 (Alaska 1991).

6. Dixon v. Freuman, 573 N.Y.S.2d (N.Y. 1991).

7. Bruce v. Memorial Mission Hospital, Inc., No. 136PA89. (1990). *Medical Malpractice Verdicts, Settlements & Experts*, 6 (8), 27-28.

8. Czubinsky v. Doctor's Hospital, 188 Cal. Rptr. 685 (Cal. App. 1983).

9. Suburban Hospital v. Hadary, 322 A.2d 258, 22 Md. App. 186 (1974).

10. Norman, Jane C. (1983). Nurses and malpractice–Just following orders isn't enough. *Legal Aspects of Medical Practice, 11* (11), 1.

Chapter 13

Confusing Licensure Issues with Malpractice

"My license is on the line!" is a concern frequently expressed by nurses who are facing difficult situations in clinical practice. Fortunately, most of the time this concern is expressed, the license is not really at issue; rather, the problem is one of malpractice or liability exposure, for which nurses seldom lose their licenses. The questions of whether the nurse will lose his or her license and whether he or she will be held liable for malpractice are completely separate and distinct and are settled in different ways.

LICENSURE

As previous chapters have discussed, nurses are liable for a malpractice event when a jury determines that they have failed to follow a reasonable, professional standard of care and that failure has resulted in harm or injury to a patient. Nurses found liable by the malpractice jury are usually practicing well within the scope of licensure; they are, however, practicing in a negligent manner. The legal basis for licensure, resides in the government's responsibility to protect the health, safety, and welfare of the public. Legislative acts to protect the public from unqualified unsafe practitioners are generally known as Practice Acts. Quite simply, then, nurses lose their licenses for the items enumerated in the Nurse Practice Acts in every state.

Licensure establishes standards for entry into practice, defines a scope of practice, and allows for disciplinary action.[1] Nurse Practice Acts define and limit the practice of nursing and so determine what constitutes unauthorized practice or practice that exceeds the scope of authority. In addition to these acts, rules and regulations may be published which tend to be more specific and provide further direction. Board rulings also help determine the scope of nursing in each state. Advisory opinions or rulings are often issued in response to a formal request by a nurse or facility for clarification of a clinical activity. In addition, the board may submit a question to a specific state agency or department such as the attorney general's department. Advisory opinions from the attorney general's office are not law but can be persuasive in a judicial proceeding.[2]

GROUNDS FOR SUSPENSION

As already stated, many situations that give nurses anxiety do not pose a threat to their licenses. For example, a hospital may decide to ask nurses to participate in a new procedure, such as performing vaginal examinations upon women in labor. Nurses, faced with this new policy, may be concerned about a perceived threat to their nursing licenses. In reality, situations like this rarely affect nurses' licenses. Nurse Practice Acts usually have a great deal of flexibility to allow for changes and growth within the nursing profession. Although some nurses would like more specific direction and guidance from the state board of nursing, it is often an advantage to the nursing profession to have this degree of flexibility. This allows the profession to develop from within as the customary standards of nursing evolve to match the evolution of health care delivery.[3]

However, if the hospital or a physician insists that a nurse perform an activity that is clearly contraindicated in a particular state's Nurse Practice Act, it is important to understand that the nurse cannot be protected from a possible loss of license by a third party. The third party does not have the ability to authorize the act that the state has not authorized. For example, if a state has determined that nurses are not permitted to accept orders for patient care from physician assistants, the hospital may not infringe upon the authority of the state and attempt, by policy, to insist that nurses follow these orders.[4]

Grounds for disciplinary action are enumerated in the Nurse Practice Acts. Although these reasons differ somewhat from state to state, the general categories usually include fraud and deceit, criminal acts, incompetence, substance abuse, mental incompetence, and unprofessional conduct.

Fraud and Deceit

The American Nurses' Association Model Act identifies fraud and deceit in securing or attempting to secure a license as well as falsification or repeated negligence in documenting patient records. In *Weber v. Colorado State Board of Nursing*,[5] a nurse was charged with violating numerous provisions of the Nurse Practice Act. The specific charges were that she had failed to furnish medical records in a timely fashion to four of her patients; that she had pleaded guilty to two felony check charges; and that she had procured her nursing license by fraud, deceit, misrepresentation, misleading omission, or material misstatements of fact by denying that she had pleaded guilty to the felonies when she applied for renewal of her license. The nurse contended that even if she had failed to handle medical records properly, that failure did not violate generally accepted standards of nursing practice. The court disagreed and pointed out that the Nurse Practice Act gives the state board of nursing the power to discipline nurses and that the handling of records constitutes an integral part of the profession of nursing and an essential element of appropriate patient care. However, the licensing board may not discipline a license who has successfully completed a deferred judgment for having been convicted of a felony or having pleaded guilty to a felony. Practicing nursing without a license is obviously a basis for disciplinary action.[6]

Unprofessional Conduct

As with any laws, the courts must determine on a case-by-case basis how Nurse Practice Acts should be interpreted. The interpretation of what constitutes "unprofessional conduct" is sometimes difficult. In *Tuma v. Board of Nursing*,[7] for example, the plaintiff appealed the 6-month suspension of her nursing license for "unprofessional conduct" proscribed by state nursing regulations. She was employed as a clinical nursing instructor at a local college, and her position included performing nursing services at Twin Falls Clinic and Hospital. The hospital complained to the state nursing board that the plaintiff had repeatedly discussed and advised cancer patients that (l) chemotherapy and other treatment prescribed by physicians would not cure them and was in fact harmful, and (2) they should discharge themselves from the hospital and undertake "natural" cancer treatment—laetrile, natural foods, and the like. The Idaho Supreme Court ordered her nursing license reinstated on the basis that the nursing board's guidelines on professional conduct were insufficient to inform the plaintiff exactly what conduct might be, in fact, unprofessional. In short, the court found a lack of concrete allegations in the record that would support the defendant's contention that the plaintiff was not a qualified and adequate practitioner of nursing.

The nurse who engages in the practice of medicine is placing the nursing license at risk. In *Hoffson v. Orentreich*,[8] the court held that the patient was entitled to a new trial of her action against a dermatologist and nurse for causing her disfiguring damages. The patient had sought treatment for loss of hair and was treated by one of the physicians in the group or by one of the nurses. During a routine visit, a registered nurse employed by the group incised and drained three acne cysts and removed blackheads from her face. The patient alleged that this resulted in disfiguring, permanent scars. She claimed that she was not examined nor seen by a physician and the procedure was not supervised. The jury returned a verdict, but the judge set it aside and dismissed the complaint. On appeal, however, the court said the complaint should not have been dismissed and that it was not utterly irrational for the jury to have reached a verdict in favor of the patient.

Having a personal relationship with a vulnerable patient is also a risky activity. In *Heinecke v. Department of Commerce*,[9] a male nurse who worked in a psychiatric unit was assigned to care for a psychiatric patient who was diagnosed with multiple personality disorder resulting from, or exacerbated by, a long history of sexual abuse, possibly including ritualistic abuse. At the time of her admission, she was also suffering from depression and was considered potentially suicidal. In addition to her other problems, her therapists were apparently concerned there might be some substance to her claim that she had been involved with a satanic cult, whose members were allegedly desirous that she return to the fold. The nurse took great interest in this patient and was convinced that she required special attention. He spent a significant amount of his free time with her at the hospital and soon learned how to "access" and communicate with some of her other personalities. Hospital administrators cautioned him that he was spending too much time with her and that she was becoming too dependent on him. Eventually, when he failed to heed these warnings and neglected his other duties, the hospital ordered him to stop seeing her. He immediately took a leave of absence and she demanded to be discharged from the hospital. He took her to his apartment, where she stayed with his wife and children until her husband moved in with them and the nurse's own marriage fell apart. Because the patient's therapist had told her and her husband that she should not become pregnant, they were practicing sexual abstinence; however, the nurse accessed a different personality and they became lovers. The patient became pregnant and her husband filed a complaint with the licensing board, which revoked the nurse's license for unprofessional conduct.

On appeal, the nurse maintained that the nurse/patient relationship had clearly ended before the sexual relationship began. He claimed that his motives were pure, and that he acted only out of love and compassion for her. Consequently, because he offered his services only as a friend and received no monetary compensation, he was exempt from the rules and regulations governing nurses generally. The appeals court found these arguments untenable and held that his actions went well beyond the bounds of compassionate service. He had met her during the course of employment and his actions were clearly related to the practice of nursing. Furthermore, he had betrayed her trust in him by exploiting her condition. In another case involving unprofessional conduct, a nurse's license was suspended for 5 years because she obtained large quantities of a controlled drug by the unauthorized use of her father's Bureau of Narcotics number. She had injected the drugs in patients as part of a weight reduction program without an order from a physician.[10]

Incompetence

Incompetence is also a reason for losing one's license. Sometimes only one occurrence can lead to suspension. In *Cafiero v. North Carolina Board of Nursing*,[11] the nurse's conduct in connecting a 2-month-old child to a monitor resulted in an electrical shock to the child and led to disciplinary action against the nurse. The nurse's license was suspended for 30 days and the decision was upheld. The violation did not require continuing conduct; a single act of negligence in certain circumstances may be sufficient. Conduct endangering the public included the act of failing to follow the head nurse's instructions to wait for assistance and then incorrectly connecting a monitor she had never used before.

Once the licensure board makes a decision that is adverse to the nurse, he or she may choose to appeal the decision to the court. The courts, reviewing decisions of administrative agencies, generally will agree with and affirm the decision, remand (send it back for further proceedings), reverse, or modify the decision. These actions will occur only if substantial rights of the petitioner may have been prejudiced. Reasons for prejudice include the findings were in violation of the U.S. Constitution, were in excess of the permitted authority of the agency, were made upon unlawful procedure or error of law, were unsupported by evidence, or were arbitrary or capricious.

Of course, sometimes a license is suspended only after repeated violations. One nurse's license was suspended for acts committed during a 3-year period. They included 17 allegations of failure to administer medication, treatment, and feedings to patients; 14 allegations of false or incorrect entries on patient records numerous allegations of sleeping on duty; 3 charges of removing patient call bells during the night; several allegations of patient abuse, including the forced feeding of one patient and hitting the stump of two amputees against their bed rails; and 1 allegation of failing to recognize that a patient was not yet dead and could be resuscitated. The nurse's termination was upheld.[12]

Substance Abuse

One of the most difficult issues facing the health care delivery system today is that of the impaired health care provider. Although technically impairment may refer to physical as well as emotional impairment, most cases today deal with impairment caused by drug or alcohol abuse.

Many state boards of nursing report chemical dependency as the leading cause of disciplinary proceedings. Since addiction often goes untreated and undetected, its reported prevalence may be low. Nevertheless, the number of nurses addicted is reported to be 10% to 12%. This means that among every 15 nurses employed in the hospital, at least 1 will have a serious alcohol- or drug-related problem. Unfortunately, the number of cases dealing with drug or alcohol abuse are increasing. Conversion of hospital drugs for one's own personal use is one example of the problem.

Identification of the impaired nurse is critical if the hospital is to protect patients from harm and itself from liability. The hospital's authority to deal with a nurse's impairment derives from its legal responsibilities, both as the nurse's employer (vicarious liability as discussed in previous chapters) and as a corporation. The corporation owes a duty to patients for the quality of care received under the doctrine of corporate liability. However, the way a hospital intervenes when there is reasonable evidence that a nurse is addicted may determine whether or not other nurses request help or decide to hide their problems. For example, impaired nurses clearly should be given an opportunity to participate in a rehabilitation program. If the price of requesting help is loss of job and/or professional license, the impaired nurse will seldom seek help. A disciplinary response to addiction also makes it difficult for peers to deal with the problem.

To help in the identification process, confidential reporting within the hospital by coworkers should be encouraged. Proof of an addiction is not necessary for such a report, but factual information resulting in a belief that a problem exists should be communicated as objectively as possible. The identity of the employee bringing forward the information should be protected from disclosure or discovery. The nurse manager's investigation either will confirm or deny the initial information. If confirmed, hospital policy will then determine appropriate action.

Nurses may fear a defamation lawsuit for filing such reports if the report turns out to be unsupported. However, as long as the nurse follows the rules and does not knowingly make false statements or intentionally intend to be malicious, a defamation lawsuit based upon the report will not be successful.[13]

If the state board has received a complaint, the board must investigate and decide whether or not to discipline. Notice must be given to the nurse stating the charges as well as the time and place of the hearing. Due process requirements include this as well as the right to cross-examine witnesses, the right to produce witnesses, the right to appear with counsel, the right to a record of the proceeding, and some form of judicial review.

NOTES

1. Northrup, Cynthia E. (1987). Legal issues in nursing (P. 405). New York: C.V. Mosby.

2. Cushing, M. Maureen. (1986, February). How courts look at Nurse Practice Acts. *American Journal of Nursing, 82,* (2), 131.

3. Fiesta, Janine, (1990). Safeguarding your nursing license. *Nursing Management, 21* (8), 20.

4. Fiesta, Janine. (1990). Safeguarding your nursing licence. *Nursing Management, 21* (8), 20–22.

5. Weber v. Colorado State Board of Nursing, 830 P.2d 1128 (Colo.1992).

6. American Nurses Association: The Nurse Practice Act, 1981.

7. Tuma v. Board of Nursing, 100 Idaho 74, 593 P.2d 711 (1979).

8. Hoffson v. Orentreich, 562 N.Y.S.2d 479 (N.Y. Sup. Ct., 1990).

9. Heinecke v. Department of Commerce, 810 P.2d 459 (Utah 1991).

10. Livingston v. Nyquist 388 N.W.2d 42 (1976).

11. Cafiero v. North Carolina Board of Nursing, 403 S.E.2d 582 (N.C. App. 1991).

12. Kibler v. State, 718 P.2d 531 (Colo. 1986).

13. Fiesta, Janine. (1990). The impaired nurse-Who is liable? *Nursing Management, 21,* (8), 20.

Chapter 14

Failing to Communicate

The most important legal duty of the nurse is the duty to communicate.[1] Whether the situation involves a nurse and a physician or a nurse and management, when the nurse cannot solve the problem, the only option is to communicate the problem to someone higher in authority. For example, when a nurse has identified a change in the patient's condition, the professional nurse will communicate that information to the physician so that appropriate treatment can be determined.

REPORTING POTENTIAL PROBLEMS

Good communications are the key to successful health care. No matter how competent the physician or the nurse, the patient's health and life are threatened by a lack of communication between health care providers.[2] In *George v. LDS Hospital*,[3] for example, the patient had a hysterectomy. The nurse expert witness stated that the nurses had breached their duty to the patient by failing to follow an order to ambulate the patient and to use incentive spirometry, by failing to perform a neurological assessment of the patient when she showed signs of respiratory distress, and by failing to notify the doctors of her deteriorating condition. The patient did not survive.

In an Illinois case a patient who was admitted for drug dependency began to suffer severe headaches, and appeared to be totally incoherent, and finally passed out on the bathroom floor. Nurses returned her to bed but did not contact a physician. No progress notes indicated that the patient had been seen from 11:00 p.m. until 7:00 a.m., when she was found dead. Death was attributed to combined drug toxicity, and the jury returned a verdict for $4 million.[4]

In *Uhr v. Lutheran General Hospital*,[5] a young girl was admitted to a hospital to have a cyst removed from her femur and to have bone tissue grafted onto the femur. During the surgery, she lost as much as 30% to 40% of her total blood volume, went into cardiac arrest, and died. In this hospital, nurses normally monitored blood loss by weighing blood from the sponges used in the surgery and relaying the information regularly to the attending anesthesiologist. The anesthesiologist testified that in this case the nurses did not properly communicate blood loss information to him. The trial court ruled against the hospital, and this verdict was affirmed by the appellate court.

Obstetrical nurses must be especially attentive to monitoring the patient's condition and communicating all relevant information to the physician. In *Bryant v. John Doe Hospital*,[6] the nurse allegedly watched

2 hours of late decelerations without notifying anyone. Following delivery, the meconium aspirator could not be found and an initial attempt at intubation was unsuccessful. A second attempt was also unsuccessful because the oxygen was not working. In addition, the failure to perform a caesarean section was alleged against the family practitioner. A $5.9 million settlement was reached. In a Wisconsin case a nurse was alleged to have failed to notify the obstetrician of the mother's complete dilation. The nurse did not explain why she did not notify the physician and admitted it was her obligation to do so.[7]

Just as nurses have a responsibility to alert the physician to a change in the patient's condition, so the physician has a responsibility to alert nurses to the fact that he or she may anticipate an emergency medical condition. In one case, for example, a 24-year-old patient was admitted with shortness of breath and chest tightness. A chest x-ray indicated air in subcutaneous neck tissues and the mediastinum. The physician placed the patient on a ventilator but did not inform anyone about the air noted and the possibility that the patient would envelop a tension pneumothorax. The physician left the hospital and the patient arrested and died. The court held that the physician should have communicated the x-ray findings to the staff.[8]

In *Gladewater Municipal Hospital v. Daniel* (1985),[9] both the nurses and the physician were found to have been negligent in failing to change a patient's bandages a sufficient number of times. The nurses were held responsible for failing to report the drainage of the wound to the physician, and the physician was held responsible for failing to properly monitor the condition of the wound. The verdict was over $100,000.

The nurse must be alert for any detail that might be important. In *Brown v. E. A. Conway Memorial Hospital*,[10] the plaintiff was stabbed in the right shoulder during a fight and was taken to the defendant's emergency room for treatment. He testified that he had been stabbed by a pocket knife with two blades and that one blade had broken off. After taking the knife away from the assailant, he gave it to his father. The plaintiff and his parents testified that the knife was shown to a hospital nurse in the emergency room. The treating physician testified that the plaintiff had told him that he had been stabbed with a short-blade penknife; however, he did not take x-rays and did not suspect that there was a foreign object under the plaintiff's skin. Approximately 2 months later, after the plaintiff experienced pain and swelling in his shoulder, a 2-inch knife blade was discovered there and removed. The treating physician and another physician both testified that they would have taken x-rays had they been informed of the broken blade. In judging this case, the court noted that a hospital has a duty to exercise that amount of care necessitated by a patient's condition, and may be held liable for the negligent conduct of all of its employees acting in the scope of their employment. From the evidence, the court concluded that the possibility that the knife blade had broken off was an important piece of information which should have been reported to the treating physician.

BEING WARY OF TELEPHONE CONVERSATIONS

A special problem with communication occurs when the telephone is involved. Everyone knows the game of sitting in a circle and starting a story. By the time the story comes around the circle, it never resembles the initial story. Similarly, when a nurse calls the doctor's office for clarification of a note or order and the physician does not come to the phone in person, a potential pitfall exists which is compounded by the number of individuals that may become involved in the communication link. For example, a nurse at a patient's bedside places a call to the physician, who is in the office, and then returns to care for the patient. The nurse's request for an order or clarification of an existing order is then communicated from the doctor's desk receptionist, to the office nurse, to the physician. The physician, now having received the communication, but not necessarily accurately, responds. The response is taken from the office nurse, through the office receptionist, to the hospital person who answers the phone on the unit. This individual then communicates the answer either directly to the nurse caring for the patient or to the charge nurse, who then communicates to the patient's nurse. Perhaps it is a miracle that more errors do not occur.

Telephone advice is especially dangerous when medication orders are communicated over the telephone. To guard against this pitfall, some hospitals prohibit telephone orders related to dangerous medications such as chemotherapy. Other hospitals do not permit the "do not resuscitate" order to be communicated by telephone, not merely because of the possibility of error but also because of the potential seriousness of the problem if the information is inaccurate. In some situations, then, orders must be signed by the physician before they are carried out. This procedure can be very important in preventing an injury. In States where physician assistants are permitted to write orders (as scribes) on the chart, the nurse may not be allowed, either under law or hospital policy, to follow the order until it is countersigned by the doctor.

In *Redford v. U.S.A.*,[11] the court awarded $170,000 to a patient who had undergone surgery for a ruptured appendix and had peritonitis. The patient attempted unsuccessfully to become pregnant and eventually had a hysterectomy based upon information given to her by her physician. The jury found that this was an unnecessary procedure for a 34-year-old patient. The patient had spoken to the physician over the telephone twice prior to the surgery, and the substance of the conversations was disputed concerning the risks and side-effects of the surgery.

How to Avoid Liability

One of the best ways to avoid liability, once again, is not only to communicate but to document one's communications. Failure to document may indicate failure to communicate. For example, in *Ketchum v. Overlake Hospital* (1991),[12] the patient had a subarachnoid hemorrhage and aneurysm. Following neurosurgery, the patient's condition deteriorated in the intensive care unit. The nurse allegedly failed to document neurological changes and to communicate these to the doctor.

Sometimes the nurse forgets to chart the "doctor notified" note. This may become a problem if the physician later testifies that the nurse did not call and the nurse testifies that the notification did occur. The jury must then evaluate the testimony, determine the credibility of the witnesses, and decide who is telling the truth. In general, a major function of the jury in the malpractice courtroom is to resolve such inconsistencies in testimony. If, however, the nurse documents that the physician was called but the physician denies this, the jury is more likely to believe the nurse's version of the events. Juries have great difficulty believing that a nurse would deliberately lie in charting on a patient's medical record.

Finally, it is important to remember that nurses are expected to use their professional judgment in the absence of specific orders, and they can be held liable for not doing so. In *Warren v. Canal*,[13] a patient who had been in a motorcycle accident had a damaged liver. A central venous pressure line was inserted but no x-ray was performed. The patient died following pain and difficulty breathing. The physician had given no specific instructions to the intensive care nurse as to whether or when he should be contacted if changes did occur. The intensive care unit charge nurse was a named defendant. The court held that, in the absence of specific medical orders, the nurse should have called the physician as soon as any other intensive care unit nurse with her experience would have called.

NOTES

1. Fiesta, Janine. (1990, February). The Nursing Shortage: Whose Liability Problem? Part II. *Nursing Management, 21* (2), 22.

2. Tammello, David. (1991, December). Failure to Document and Communicate Catastrophic Results. *Regan Report on Nursing Law, 31* (7), 1.

3. George v. LDS Hospital, 797 P.2d 1117 (Utah 1990).

4. Harrington v. Rush-Presbytarian, St. Luke's Hospital, 569 N.E. 2d 15 (Ill. 1990).

5. Uhr v. Lutheran General Hospital, No. 1-87-3534 (Ill. 1992).

6. Bryant v. John Doe Hospital and John Doe, M.D. (1992). *Medical Malpractice Verdicts, Settlements & Experts, 8* (1), 35.

7. E.M.D. v. Mutual of Omaha, No. 88-CV-18418 (Wis. 1992).

8. Rixey v. West Paces Ferry Hospital, Inc. 916 F.2d 608 (Ga. 1990).

9. Gladewater Municipal Hospital v. Daniel 694 S.W.2d 619 (Tex. 1985).

10. Brown v. E.A. Conway Memorial Hospital, W.L. 226557 (La. Ct. App. 1991).

11. Redford v. U.S.A., District of Columbia, No. 89-2324. (1992). *Medical Malpractice Verdicts, Settlements & Experts, 8* (12), 22.

12. Ketchum v. Overlake Hospital, 804 P.2d 1283 (Wash. 1991).

13. Warren v. Canal, 300 S.E.2d 557 (N.C. 1988).

Failing to Monitor and Assess

Although nurses often feel they are responsible for everything that happens to their patients, this is not realistic and does not reflect liability principles. Every employee is responsible for his or her own actions; therefore, everyone is personally accountable for what he or she does or fails to do. However, because nurses are with the patient on a more constant basis than any other health care provider, they do have a specific legal duty to monitor and assess the patient's clinical condition. Nurses care for the patient on a 24-hour basis; the physician sees the patient only a short period of time during that 24-hour interval. Therefore, if the patient's condition worsens, the nurse must be able to assess that change and notify the physician that the patient may need medical intervention.

As nurses have grown in their professionalism, legal accountability has correspondingly increased, and nurses are increasingly finding themselves **named defendants** in malpractice cases. This was not so in earlier cases, even when the actions of the nurse were the issue, because nurses were not considered truly independent practitioners. The perception was that the nurse functioned as the handmaiden of the physician or as the employee of the hospital, present to follow doctors' orders or hospital policy without thought or question. Clearly, that is no longer the perception and, arguably, was never a valid belief. The nurse is now expected to exercise independent judgment and to therefore assume accountability if the judgment or assessment is negligent.

It is important to understand that such negligence is always measured prospectively rather than by hindsight. That is, when the jury is determining whether or not the nurse functioned according to a reasonable standard of care, the perspective is not one of looking backward, but of looking forward. On the basis of the available information at the time, did the nurse make a reasonable judgment or assessment of the patient?

MONITORING AGENCY NURSES

For the nurse manager, an important responsibility is monitoring the performance of agency nurses, who have been used more frequently as nursing shortages have become more common. The question is, how accountable is the nurse manager for the actions of these nurses? In the past, hospital staff who were not employed by the hospital were viewed as independent contractors. Private-duty nurses fell into this category, as well as attending fee-for-service physicians. The hospital traditionally was not held liable for the actions of independent contractors. Since the registry listing the available private-duty nurses also was not the employer of the nurse, the registry was not in a position of liability based upon principles of vicarious liability (see Chapter 4).[1]

Recently, however, the courts have begun to whittle away at the principle of no liability for the acts of independent contractors, and legal cases addressing this issue are beginning to appear. One innovative legal theory that has been used is the concept of **ostensible agency** or **apparent authority**. This concept applies when a patient may reasonably believe that a health care provider is an employee of the hospital—in other words, when there is no way for a patient to determine that the health care provider is *not* an employee of the hospital. Therefore, if the nurse *appears* to be an employee of the institution, he or she may in fact be considered as an employee.

In *Williams v. St. Claire Medical Center*,[2] the court questioned whether vicarious liability should be imposed upon a hospital for the negligence of independent staff personnel under the doctrine of apparent authority or ostensible agency. A teenage male patient who was admitted for an arthroscopy suffered permanent brain damage while being administered general anesthesia. All anesthesia at the hospital was administered by nurse anesthetists who were not employees of the hospital but were employed by a professional service corporation. The nurse who administered anesthesia to the patient was not certified at the time of the incident, had graduated from nurse anesthetist school only 1 month prior to the incident, and had not yet taken the examination to obtain certification. He had received temporary staff privileges limited to instances when he was under supervision of a certified registered nurse anesthetist. The hospital's published anesthesia policies required supervision, but the nurse administered anesthesia in this case without it.

The injured plaintiff argued that the hospital had breached its duty to him by failing to enforce its own rules and regulations. The hospital argued that it had no duty to supervise the nurse anesthetist, a nonemployee, and that the patient was a private patient of the orthopedic surgeon rather than a patient of the hospital, and therefore the hospital had no duty to enforce its policies on his behalf. The court stated that no reason existed to distinguish the hospital's responsibility to administer and enforce its policies based upon how the patient initially came to the hospital (private patient versus emergency care). Since the patient must accept all rules and regulations of the hospital, he should be able to expect that the hospital will follow its own rules established for this case. In addition, the patient alleged that he had no reason to believe that the nurse anesthetist was anything other than an employee of the hospital.[3]

Since hospitals can be held liable, nurse managers may be placed in a secondary liability position for agency nurses just as for their own nursing staff. That is, if they know that a registry nurse is incompetent and fail to act upon that knowledge, they may be held liable for not taking action. Nurse managers have a legal duty to communicate any available information to the registry-employer of the nurse, and registry personnel must be screened as carefully as other hospital-employed nurses. In other words, a critical need for nurses will not justify the failure to exercise reasonable care in selecting registry or other temporary nurses.[4] This was shown in Florida, where the court held that the hospital, not the registry, could be held liable for the negligent acts of such personnel.[5]

This does not mean, however, that agency nurses themselves will not be held liable. In one case, for example, an adult juvenile diabetic was hospitalized in critical condition. The nurse administered Valium but failed to monitor the patient's vital signs and she went into cardiac arrest. The jury returned a verdict of $300,000.[6] The nurse was a named defendant and the agency was also sued.

MONITORING PATIENTS

Obviously, the most important duty is to monitor patients. The failure to monitor can occur with all types of nursing procedures, from the simple to the most complex.

Failure to monitor blood pressure and respiration was a part of the claim in a Texas case that resulted in a settlement over $1 million.[7] A bright, popular high school student who had been involved in a motor vehicle accident was taken to the hospital with tenderness in the right upper quadrant. Over the course of 7 hours, he bled to death. The parents contended that the hospital and its staff were negligent in failing to ascertain the decedent's condition and that they negligently failed to provide care necessary to stop bleeding, to provide blood transfusion to replace lost blood, to monitor blood pressure and respirations, to transfer the decedent to the intensive care unit at an earlier time, to transfer the patient to a better equipped hospital, and to treat the chest trauma.

As this case shows, in many malpractice cases the list of allegations is lengthy. The disastrous result occurring to the patient when malpractice has occurred is often the result of a number of errors caused by not just one but several individuals. For example, the classic risk management nightmare is a mix-up because patients have the same name. In this case, failure to monitor the identity of the patient may be a major problem. The wrong patient having the wrong surgery is a vivid example of a number of individuals failing to meet a reasonable standard of care because more than one person is responsible for correctly identifying patients for surgery. One way to avoid this pitfall is to highlight the patients with the same name who appear on the operating room schedule. The admitting department should attempt to place such patients in different clinical units.

In one case illustrating a mix-up, the patient was ordered a computerized axial tomography scan with contrast. The plaintiff claimed that the employees gave the decedent contrast intended for a different patient with the same name. The decedent, who was 20 years younger than the other man, began to have an anaphylactic reaction to the dye within 4 minutes, and he died 5 days later. The jury returned a $5.75 million verdict.[8]

In a Florida case, a woman died the day after surgery because a breathing tube was negligently removed. The family was awarded almost $60,000, most of which would go to the diabetic daughter, who was greatly dependent upon her 51-year-old mother. Before the award could be paid, however, the daughter died when mistakenly injected with potassium instead of a saline solution. She was 26 years old. The anesthesiologist involved in the mother's care surrendered his license due to chemical abuse.[9]

Failure to monitor for compartment syndrome is a common allegation in malpractice cases. In a pediatric case, the jury awarded almost $500,000.[10] A 4-year-old girl went to the hospital for hip surgery, after which she developed compartment syndrome. Evidence was presented at trial that the nursing staff did not properly monitor the patient, that they did not obtain the equipment needed to test quickly enough, that the nurses did not know what equipment was needed, and that neither the nurses nor the doctors knew where the equipment was located.

Failure to monitor for fetal distress is a common allegation in obstetric malpractice cases. In *Fairfax Hospital System, Inc. v. McCarty*,[11] a labor and delivery room nurse was found negligent for failing to monitor the patient during a crucial 10-minute period after signs of fetal distress were already apparent. The attending physician testified that if he had been told of the patient's condition in time, he would have intervened sooner and perhaps prevented the catastrophic injury prior to birth. The jury awarded in excess of $3.5 million.

In *Olsen v. Humana, Inc.,*[12] a Kansas jury awarded $15 million, including $8.8 million in punitive damages, against a hospital corporation and an obstetrician following the birth of an infant who sustained severe brain damage as a result of the defendant's failure to respond adequately to fetal distress. The bulk of the punitive damages award was allocated against the hospital's parent corporation for failing to hire a competent and well-trained nursing staff. The nurse who attended the mother during labor was not trained to read the electronic fetal heart monitoring system and failed to detect the distressed fetal heart rate. In addition, the physician who delivered the infant failed to properly resuscitate the infant because he lacked adequate training in resuscitation of neonates.

In the nursery, failure to monitor oxygen levels to premature infants was once a more frequent allegation against nurses than it is now, but such problems still occur. In *Willis v. El Camino Hospital,*[13] a settlement worth over $4 million was reached in a lawsuit charging nurses with negligence in the administration of oxygen to twins born 9 weeks premature. They sustained total blindness because of retrolental fibroplasia. The lawsuit charged the pediatrician with failure to monitor blood gases during the last 9 days of oxygen administration and failure to respond appropriately to abnormally high blood gases as reflected in the levels obtained during the first 7 days of oxygen administration. The hospital was sued for the negligence of its nurses in failing to adhere to protocols for monitoring oxygen levels, failing to advise the doctor that excessive levels of oxygen were being administered, and failing to independently reduce the amount of oxygen being administered.

In the recovery room or postanesthesia care unit (PACU), monitoring is the principal activity of the nurse. Therefore, failure to monitor in this setting is an extremely serious malpractice liability exposure. A 1978 study on malpractice claims conducted by the National Association of Insurance Commissioners rates the recovery room as having the highest percentage of injuries and claims of all the hospital areas.[14]

In one case, the jury returned a $550,000 verdict against four recovery room nurses and a patient's cardiologist for death resulting from mismanagement of a patient's postoperative recovery room care.[15] The patient, who was undergoing surgical closure of a colostomy, had premature ventricular contractions (PVCs) after anesthesia was administered. The consulting cardiologist, who was called by the surgeon, administered lidocaine and cleared the patient for the 2-hour surgery. The patient continued to exhibit PVCs while she was in the recovery room. Approximately 3 hours after the surgery, she experienced a cardiac arrest, which caused hypoxic brain damage that led to her death 2 weeks later. The family brought suit against the nurses for failing to perform one-to-one monitoring of the patient. The evidence at trial established that the head nurse had interpreted the written protocols as requiring continual cardiac monitoring only until the patient was stabilized. The team leader had administered 50 mg. of Demerol about 45 minutes prior to the cardiac arrest, but she failed to detect the clinically adverse reaction to the drug that resulted in cardiac arrest. The nurse who was providing one-to-one care of the patient was diverted from her task, and the cardiac arrest went undiagnosed and untreated for 5 to 10 minutes. The jury ruled that the head nurse and team leader were each 45% liable, and the nurse who was responsible for one-to-one monitoring was 5% liable. The cardiologist was 5% liable for negligently clearing the patient for major surgery and for failing to properly follow the postoperative recovery room course.

In *Sanchez v. Bay General Hospital*,[16] a woman underwent an elective laminectomy. After being transferred to the recovery room, she vomited. For the 2 hours she remained in the recovery room, she appeared to be satisfactorily recovering. Her vital signs, which were taken every 15 minutes, appeared normal.

Various nurses took the patient's vital signs at 15-minute intervals. But they didn't compare their readings with previous ones. They also ignored warnings from her visitors that she was vomiting constantly and having trouble breathing.

The patient went into cardiac arrest; the unit nurses called a code. None of them knew how to perform cardiopulmonary resuscitation (CPR), however, so it wasn't begun until an ED doctor reached the unit. All the emergency medications were administered through the atrial catheter, directly into her heart. The resuscitation attempt failed and she remained in a vegetative state until her death, 2 months later.

The court pointed out the following omissions of the nursing staff: no examination of the patient's pupils was done on her arrival in the ward; no suctioning equipment was ordered, "though her medical chart, had it been reviewed, reflected she was vomiting while in the recovery room"; no comparison was made of the patient's vital signs in the recovery room and those taken at 3:30 P.M. which showed a significant decrease; vital signs were not taken at an increased interval there-after; no medication checks were undertaken; no neurological examination was done; no reflexes were tested; the nursing staff failed to realize the existence of the atrial catheter; no supervisory nurse or physician was notified of the deteriorating vital signs; requests by friends and family went ignored; and no report was made to the incoming shift about the patient's condition.

Although several family members reported that the patient was vomiting, they were told that everything had been taken care of and that they could give the patient water, in spite of an order directing that no water be given. No physician or supervisor was contacted, and the patient's chart was never consulted.

The patient was in a vegetative state until she died as the result of more nursing negligence. The nursing staff failed to properly inflate and care for the balloon cushion on the cuff of the tracheostomy tube.

As the result of this failure, the cuff of the tracheostomy tube gradually worked its way through the posterior of the trachea, eroded part of the left anterior aspect of the thoracic vertebrae, and eroded laterally on the right side of the innominate artery. When this artery eroded, the patient bled to death.

NOTES

1. Restatement (second) of Torts 429 (1960).

2 Williams v. St. Claire. Medical Center, 657 S.W.2d 590 (Kent. 1983).

3. Mancini, Marguerite R., and Alice T. Gale. (1981). Emergency Care and the Law (P.22). Rockville, Maryland: Aspen Publications.

4. ECRI, (1988, October) The nursing shortage: A liability threat, *Hospital Risk Control Update.*

5. Robison v. Faine, 525 S.2d 903 (Fla. 1988).

6. Martinez v. St. Josephs Hospital and Medical Center, Med. Pro., Inc. and Kopischke, RN, No. 88-31358. (1990). *Medical Malpractice Verdicts, Settlements & Experts, 6* (10), 29.

7. Barton v. AMI Park Place Hospital et al., No. 909-066318 (1992). *Medical Malpractice Verdicts, Settlements & Experts, 8* (9), 18.

8. Siegel v. Computerized Scanning Associates and Belt, M.D. (1992). *Medical Malpractice Verdicts, Settlements & Experts, 8* (3), 52.

9. Pendley v. Shands et al. (1992). *Medical Malpractice Verdicts, Settlements & Experts, 8* (1), 3-4.

10. Pirkov-Middaugh v. Gillette Children's Hospital, No. C9-91-526 (Minn. 1991).

11. Fairfax Hospital System, Inc. v. McCarty, 419 S.E.2d 621 (Va. 1992).

12. Olsen v. Humana, Inc., No. 107480, Johnson County Dist. Ct. (Kan. 1984).

13. Willis v. El Camino Hospital, No. 468929, Santa Clara Sup. Ct. Cal., Reported in 28 ATLA L.Rep. 227 (June 1985).

14. Torbert v. Befeler, No. L-17463-81, Union Cty. Sup. Ct. (April 25, 1985), reported in, 28 ATLA L.Rep. 469 (December 1985).

15. Williams v. Fort Worth Children's Medical Center, 352-88610-85. (1990). *Medical Malpractice Verticts, Settlements & Experts, 6* (5), 29.

16. Sanchez v. Bay General Hospital, 172 CA. Rptr.342 (Cal. App. 1981).

Chapter 16

Not Listening

Failure to communicate was addressed as a previous pitfall, but it is erroneous to think of communication as only talking. Listening is such an important part of communication that not doing it comes a separate pitfall. Failure to listen includes ignoring patient requests for assistance, ignoring information provided by patients and families, as well as ignoring patient's wishes and feelings.

LISTENING TO INFORMATION

For whatever the reason, sometimes nurses simply do not listen to what patients explicitly tell them. In *Parker v. Bulloch County Hospital Authority*,[1] the plaintiff, a recovering surgery patient, fell while taking a shower at the hospital. In her complaint, she stated that she had complained of dizziness as an employee of the hospital helped her into the shower, but her statement was ignored. The court noted that expert testimony was required to establish whether permitting the patient to shower alone constituted negligence.

In *Manning v. Twin Falls Clinic and Hospital*[2] a decision was made by hospital staff to move the patient to a private room. At the time the treating physician estimated that the patient had only 24 hours to live. Preparatory to the move, his supplemental oxygen was temporarily disconnected. Although the family members present strenuously urged that he be given a portable oxygen unit during the move, the nurse declined to do so because of the relatively short distance of the transfer. His bed was pushed no more than 15 feet when his condition suddenly worsened. Resuscitation efforts were attempted and a doctor was summoned. However, when he was identified as a "no code" patient, the doctor provided no treatment and the patient died shortly thereafter. The punitive damage award of $300,000 against the nurse was upheld based upon the jury's belief that the nurse's conduct was an extreme deviation from the standard of care. Punitive damages were also awarded by the jury against the hospital of $180,000; however, the court on appeal found evidence that shortly after this incident the hospital adopted a policy requiring all patients on supplemental oxygen to be moved with oxygen in place. The court found that this subsequent action of the hospital indicated that the hospital did not agree with the nurse's action. The message was clear: even though nurses testified that the procedure was always done this way, that fact is no defense when the procedure harms a patient. In addition, insensitive conduct toward the family of a very ill patient can be considered extreme and outrageous conduct for which damages for emotional distress can be assessed.[3]

In *Lopez v. Southwest Community Health Service*,[4] the jury' found that the negligence of nurses influenced the physician's decision to proceed with delivery. After experiencing pain at home, the patient, who was 28 weeks pregnant, called her physicians office. The office nurse informed the hospital that the patient was on her way and having contractions. This was an assumption by the nurse or an incorrect nursing judgment. The first nurse encountered by the patient declined to examine the patient because of a lack of experience. A second hospital nurse examined her and determined that she was 10 cm dilated and ready to deliver. Neither nurse took a history, nor did they talk to her. If the nurses had talked to (or listened to) the patient, they would have learned that neither the patient nor her mother believed she was in labor. The physician and hospital contended that the patient was in labor with bulging membranes and the fetus was in a transverse position. The physician broke the amniotic sac and delivered the baby, who is now a quadriplegic, deaf, blind, mute, and brain damaged. The jury believed that not only did the nurses fall to communicate with the patient, but that their communication with the physician adversely influenced decisions regarding care of the patient, although he testified to the contrary. The jury found 70% liability against the physician and 30% against the hospital.

Of course, sometimes the physician does not listen. In one case, the patient was admitted to the hospital to deliver her baby, the plaintiff. The attending physicians continued to administer drugs to the mother to induce labor even though the fetal monitor revealed fetal distress for 6 hours. A cesarean section was not performed, despite testimony that a nurse pleaded with the physicians to perform one. When the plaintiff was finally ready to be delivered, no physician was around and the nurse had to handle the birth alone. The trauma of the incident and the fetal distress caused the plaintiff (now 16) to suffer profound brain damage and to require around-the-clock nursing care. The child has lived in a near vegetative state since her birth and is confined to a nursing home. The parties settled for $6.8 million.[5]

LISTENING TO FEELINGS

In addition to listening to patients, nurses need to be careful in responding to patients. Sometimes the patient perceives insensitivity through the terms used by health care providers. In these cases the nurse's inappropriate response to the patient's comments may be a liability issue.

Unfortunately, some cases involve clearly inappropriate responses and gross insensitivity. For example, in one case a $450,000 jury award was upheld and the hospital held liable for negligence because a hospital employee told a patient that if he did not like the way the hospital was run he could leave. Failure to diagnose spinal meningitis occurred because the patient left. The court said that no matter how the patient acts, employees must respond as professionals.[6] In another case the nurse allegedly called a patient who was receiving dialysis a "black son of a bitch"; the jury awarded $4,500.[7] In yet another case, a nurse who told a patient in labor to "shut up" because she was disturbing other patients found herself involved as a defendant. The fetus was delivered and pronounced dead. When a nurse wrapped the deceased baby in a sheet, the patient asked where the nurse was taking the baby. The patient said the nurse responded by saying "We dispose of them right here at the hospital." The patient sued for outrageous conduct by insensitive nurses.[8]

Sometimes health care personnel feel threatened by the situation or the patient. In one instance, a patient's wife complained about a long delay in obtaining treatment and told the nursing supervisor in the intensive care unit that she might consult an attorney. The nurse warned, "If you get an attorney your husband's name will be placed on a computer and all the doctors and hospitals in this area will know about him and no one will take him as a patient." The patient had chest pains in the emergency room and delay in treatment and suffered a heart attack.[9]

In situations such as these, sometimes an immediate oral expression of concern is necessary. For example, assume that a physician performs surgery to resect a 10-inch segment of a patient's small intestine that must be removed because of blockages caused by adhesions and disease. During the operation, a portion of good small intestine is accidentally cut, resulting in the need to resect another 2 inches of good bowel.

This problem must be disclosed to the patient or an appropriate family member as soon as practicable, usually in the patient's hospital room. But there are right ways and wrong ways to give this information. One wrong way to explain is to say, "I have to tell you I made a mistake. While resecting your bowel I accidentally cut a nearby section of good intestine and therefore I had to do a second resection." Another incorrect approach is to say, "Hey, I'm really sorry, but we made a little goof and had to take some extra intestine." A better approach is this:

During surgery we ran into a complication, but it's not serious. While removing the diseased part of your intestine a section of good intestine that was pushed up under the bad part was cut, and so we had to make a second resection to remove a 2-inch section of the intestine around the cut. This is unfortunate, but it's often impossible to clearly see all the intestines since they are pushing against each other. This should not cause you any problems, now or in the future, but I noted it in your chart so we can keep an eye on it and make absolutely sure no problems ever develop. Now, do you have any questions—anything more I can explain?[10]

In these situations, nurses and doctors should not try to be amateur lawyers by making statements they think will technically absolve them from an admission of legal liability. For instance, they should not say or write, "Although this is not an admission of liability or fault, I am sorry that we will have to operate again." Such a clumsy attempt will not help in court, and might actually give the patient or the patient's family the idea of taking legal action.[11]

One thing that must be done is to make a notation in the patient's chart stating that the medical condition and outcome was discussed and explain. A brief summary of the explanation given should also be placed into the notes. Although this takes time, it can be very useful, both in showing what explanation was given and in summarizing the facts of the case. If a lawsuit is filed, this can help avoid the problem physicians and nurses have in remembering what was done years ago.[12]

Whenever an injury occurs, it is also important to apologize. An apology is not the same thing as admitting blame, and one should never underestimate its value. Though some might ask, why apologize? An equally good question is, why not? For example, a nurse who says, "I was negligent, I administered the wrong medication," should also say, " I am sorry for what has happened to you" and *stop there*. It is not necessary and in fact dangerous to blame others: "Nurse 'X' was negligent because the IV had run out." Is an inappropriate comment. As explained earlier, admitting to "negligent" conduct is not accurate because negligence is a legal term and only a jury can determine if negligence has occurred.

In some instances it is not appropriate to send a bill to a patient if you believe the patient is considering a malpractice suit or if the patient has a negative outcome that he or she did not expect. The patient's definition of what is expected is not necessarily identical to the health care provider's definition. Forgiveness of bills or reimbursement is not an admission of liability and is not introduced in court in many states. Even if it is, it serves to mitigate or decrease the financial harm suffered by the patient.

In conclusion, it is possible to express concern for the patient without admitting legal liability. Refusal to acknowledge poor results may be the very thing that causes a patient or family to visit an attorney. An appropriate response to a problem should express compassion and concern, yet not increase liability exposure. In one instance, a baby died during delivery and the physician wrote a letter of sympathy to the family in which he said, "I'm horrified that your child was lost during delivery. I have examined my conscience and can only express my sorrow. I hope I have learned enough from this case so that this will never happen again in my practice." This physician could have more safely written, "I am greatly distressed for you and your family. I can only imagine what all of you must feel. I know it's not enough to say that medicine is not an exact science, or that regardless of the care used, some babies will always be delivered stillborn, even if this is true. If there is anything I can do to aid you and your family in this time of need, please let me know."[13] In saying this the physician is putting the emphasis on how he can help the family rather than on his own incompetence. The same kind of communication can be used by nurses in many situations.

NOTES

1. Parker v. Bulloch County Hospital Authority, A90A0762. (1990). *Medical Malpractice Verdicts, Settlements & Experts, 6* (10), 28.

2. Manning v. Twin Falls Clinic and Hospital, 830 P.2d 1185 (Idaho 1992).

3. Horty, John, Editor. (1992, October/November). Punitive damages awarded against L.P.N., *Patient Care Law*, An Action-Kit Publication, 4.

4. Lopez v. Southwest Community Health Service, 833 P.2d 1183 (N. Mex. 1992)

5. Herron v. Northwest Community Hospital, Emergency Medical Services Associates et al., Cook County Il. (1992). *Medical Malpractice Verdicts, Settlements & Experts, 8* (10), 33.

6. Baptist Memorial Hospital v. Bowen, 591 So.2d 74 (Ala. 1991).

7. Hall v. Bio-Medical Application, Inc., 671 F.2d 300 (8th Cir. 1982).

8. Humana of Kentucky v. Seitz, 796 S.W.1 (1990).

9. Hanusek v. Southern Maine Medical Center, 584 A.2d 634 (Maine 1990).

10. Frierson, James G. (1990). Expressing concern for the patient without admitting legal liability. *Journal of the Tennessee Medical Association, 83* (8), 409–411.

11. Ibid.

12. Griffith, James. (1989). Why I tell good doctors to settle malpractice claims. *Medical Economics, 16*, 54-58.

13. Frierson, James (1990). Expressing concern for the patient without admitting legal liability. *Journal of the Tennessee Medical Association, 83*, 409–411.

Chapter 17

Neglecting to Follow Risk Management Principles

Throughout most of their legal history, hospitals were considered charitable enterprises, and were therefore immune from legal suits stemming from patient injuries. Furthermore, hospitals were regarded by the courts as having little control over, and consequently little responsibility for, the quality of medical services provided to their patients.

Since the late 1950s, however, courts have extended the legal responsibilities of the hospital beyond ensuring the quality of the physical facilities and equipment. Under the legal doctrine of **respondeat superior** (also discussed in Chapter 4), hospitals were held accountable for the negligent acts of employees and agents. More recent court decisions have expanded the hospital's direct obligation to ensure not only a proper level of hospital management and operations and the appropriate conduct of employees and agents, but also the clinical competence and performance of all practitioners granted clinical privileges. This developing doctrine of **corporate liability** has major consequences for the nursing profession. It is now the nurse's responsibility to communicate significant management information such as physician, staffing, and equipment problems.

Another factor cited for the increasing vulnerability of hospitals has been the legal concept of **joint and several liability**, still used in most states. Under this concept, any one of the defendants in a multidefendant suit, even if only marginally involved, may be required to pay the full amount of the award if codefendants are unable to pay. When this rule applies, hospitals may be perceived as "deep pocket" defendants, since they usually carry higher limits of liability coverage than individual members of their medical staffs. In addition, there is the perception that corporate defendants are likely to pay more than individual defendants in similar cases, particularly in cases involving severely injured plaintiffs.

Some hospitals have reacted to increasing malpractice problems by eliminating or curtailing higher risk services such as obstetrics. Such a strategy, however, reduces hospital admissions and revenues, and may limit community access to needed services. A second and more common approach has been to increase malpractice insurance coverage limits and/or to alter the form of coverage—most often to a combination of purchased insurance from an outside insurance company and self-insurance. These changes, particularly during the mid-1980s, usually resulted in more expenses paid for liability coverage during a period when both patient admissions and revenues were falling. A third strategy has been to institute management programs to control hospital risk and prevent malpractice claims.

OBJECTIVES OF RISK MANAGEMENT

Hospital risk management is a systematic program designed to reduce preventable injuries and accidents and to minimize financial loss to the institution. Traditionally, these programs in many hospitals have concentrated on maintaining and improving facilities and equipment as well as protecting employee, visitor, and patient safety. It has become increasingly clear, however, that the greatest risk of claims against hospitals comes from patient care in clinical areas such as general surgery and obstetrics. This recognition has broadened the traditional focus to include activities designed to identify, evaluate, and reduce the risk of patient injury associated with clinical care.

Some of the primary objectives of clinical risk management programs are (l) to reduce the frequency of preventable adverse occurrences that lead to liability claims by maintaining or improving the quality of care; (2) to reduce the probability of a claim being filed after an adverse event has occurred through prompt identification and follow-up; and (3) to help control the costs of those claims that do emerge through early identification and intervention with the patient and/or family. The preventive aspects of risk management should be emphasized: preventing the patient or other party from being angry or hostile, preventing the patient from being injured, preventing the patient from filing a malpractice claim, preventing a filed claim from proceeding to litigation, and preventing the hospital's loss of a lawsuit.

Crucial to clinical risk management programs are methods for identifying adverse patient events. This concern has led to the development of early warning systems. A variety of approaches are used for flagging incidents that under optimal conditions are not a normal consequence of a patient's disease or treatment and that may (but do not necessarily) represent or result from a provider's breach of the standard of care or duty owed to the patient.

Such early warning systems are critical for at least two reasons. First, they make possible early investigation and intervention, enabling hospital personnel to avoid or at least reduce the likelihood of adverse consequences and potential liability exposure. Second, the information provided by such reporting systems allows for the creation of data bases that may help identify strategies to prevent repeated occurrences.

The most common early warning systems rely on occurrence (that is, clinical incident) reporting and/or occurrence screening for adverse event detection. In **occurrence reporting**, certain criteria serve as guidelines for defining specific adverse events that must be reported by physicians and/or hospital staff either at the time they are observed or shortly thereafter. Examples of such criteria might include the unplanned return of a patient to the operating room or a medication error requiring intervention. By contrast, **occurrence screening** techniques flag adverse events through a review of either all or some of the medical charts. These reviews use generic criteria (such as the presence of hospital-acquired infection or medication error) and/or specialty- or service-specific criteria (such as an incorrect sponge count during surgery) for more focused review. Substantial efforts during the past decade have been invested in developing both generic and focused criteria for reporting and screening systems, and there is a growing amount of literature documenting and comparing the effectiveness of various approaches.[1]

Also emphasized in the risk management literature is the importance of organizational structure and the commitment of key groups. Occurrence screening identifies much useful information, but the effort is not effective if there is no strong organizational structure for dealing with the information. The participation of physicians, support from clinical chiefs of service (particularly those in the high-risk areas of surgery, emergency services, and obstetrics), cooperation between risk management and quality assurance program staff, and strong oversight and commitment of resources by the governing board are all regarded as critical elements for success. It is very important to notify the clinical chairperson of adverse medical events. The clinical chairperson may then talk with the physician involved, or perhaps study the medical records more closely. More formally, on the basis of a particularly serious event or pattern of incidents, a clinical chairperson may recommend remedial education, required proctoring, or the restriction of privileges.

RISK MANAGEMENT AND QUALITY ASSURANCE

In many hospitals, the risk management program is coordinated with the **quality assurance** program to ensure that the legal duty to provide reasonable care is fulfilled. Each system aims at a different aspect of patient care delivery. Quality assurance focuses on the role of the health care provider, and risk management focuses on the perception of patients and families. Quality assurance measures conduct according to the institution's quality standards, and risk management measures the same conduct according to the reasonable standards of care to which pertinent scientific literature and experienced practitioners can attest.

Since a hospital's reputation for safe, reliable, effective service is its primary guard against liability claims, systematic, well-coordinated quality assurance and risk management programs publicly demonstrate that the hospital is overseeing institutional services in a legally responsible manner. By promoting predictable, sound practices, quality assurance departments shape public expectations and perceptions and prevent liability claims. And by promptly handling complaints which do arise, risk managers contain the damage and minimize liability claims.

Receiving pertinent, significant information on patient care is crucial to the success of both programs. Incident reports were primary sources of information in the earlier days of risk management. Because the phrase *incident report* acquired many threatening connotations, however, different terms have replaced it. Instead of *incident*, the words *occurrence*, *situation*, or *event* are now being used. In this content, an event is "any happening which is not consistent with the routine operation of the facility or the routine care of a particular patient. It may be an accident or a situation which might result in an accident. This might involve patient, visitor, volunteer."[2] Although these reports are primarily risk management tools, they are also important for quality assurance, which is interested in trends or repeated events that prevent the hospital from rendering excellent care. Therefore, both departments will share significant information from these reports.

There are also many other resources which can alert risk and quality assurance managers to problems that require prompt attention. Patient complaints to the patient representatives' office are a highly significant source of information, since, as stated before, the primary cause of malpractice claims is not necessarily malpractice, but an unhappy patient or family. A dissatisfied health care consumer will visit an attorney's office to determine whether a malpractice claim can be initiated. Patient representatives are experienced at identifying patients who are likely to seek legal recourse. Following an incident, they also have an important role in maintaining direct communications with the patient and family. Generally, they are not responsible for informing patients about incidents: that is usually the duty of the physicians or the nurses who were actually caring for the patient when the cause for complaint took place.

The business office is also responsible for reporting patient complaints to risk management. Sometimes, only when the bill for services has been received do patients decide they have a complaint about the manner in which those services were rendered.

When potential litigants have not been identified in the course of operations and billing, the first notice of the patient's dissatisfaction may be a request to the medical records department for a copy of the medical records. In most states patients no longer need to initiate malpractice suits to obtain a copy of their own medical record. Therefore, establishing a regular mechanism for the medical records department to report an attorney's requests to the risk management department is essential to managing malpractice problems.

Once notice of a potential or actual claim has been received, the risk manager notifies the medical records and the hospital's insurance carrier. Medical records will make copies of the medical record and file the original records separately under special security arrangements. Procedures may vary from place to place, but controlling the ability to tamper with or alter the medical record is the primary objective.

Any claim notice should also trigger a quality assurance/peer review of the medical record. The chairperson of the department, quality assurance department, or, in some cases, an external reviewer may conduct this review. Its purpose is to measure the health care provider's conduct against the reasonable, professional standards of conduct for the particular situation. Such an analysis is crucial because the defendant's behavior will be measured against this standard. This review helps the risk manager investigate the claim's merit.

The "reasonable professional standard" required for a successful defense is not necessarily the same as the institution's optimal, high-quality standard. This review of the record serves the additional purpose of helping to define the hospital's responsibility for care in particular situations. To obtain this knowledge, the quality assurance office may decide to study the medical records of other patients cared for by a particular health care provider besides the patient making the claim.

Risk management and quality assurance often combine educational efforts. Education may be directed to a specific employee or physician who has been identified by either system as having a particular problem. More frequently, however, educational efforts are aimed at a larger audience. Teaching new residents and nurses about malpractice claims, risk management, and quality assurance is a high priority. Hospital orientation programs should introduce all new employees to the principles of risk management and quality assurance and instruct them in their particular reporting obligations and channels. Everyone should also understand that risk management is not a punitive system. This is essential because risk management cannot function adequately unless all significant information finds its way into suitable reporting channels. Social workers, pastors, volunteers, and escorts who have identified highly dissatisfied patients are all important sources of information, as are reports from engineering about the safety of the environment and reports from purchasing, biomedical engineering, and pharmacy on the safety and adequacy of products and equipment.

As much as possible, of course, reports must be documented. Thorough, consistent documentation is a vital consideration in both risk management and quality assurance. This means, for nurses, that writing in a patient's chart should be taken as seriously as directly caring for them.[3] The documentation—or absence of documentation—in the patient's medical record is crucial to evaluating defensibility of a case, or to evaluating whether a reasonable standard of care was followed. For the quality assurance program, the medical record's primary function is to provide an ongoing record of care on which medical treatment decisions are based.[4]

Any event which affects the course of patient care should be charted on the patient's medical record. However, the words *incident report filed* should not be recorded there, since this is just the information that will be used to alert the risk manager that a particular event has taken place. In many situations, the person initiating the actual incident report will duplicate what has already been charted on the patient's medical record.

Nurses can do several things to avoid potential litigation, some of which have been described in previous chapters. One of the simplest and most effective preventive measures is to establish sound relationships with patients and their families. Being consistent and including the patient and family in discussions and decisions regarding care are essential to developing these relationships. Nurses should establish open communication and trust, because patients and their families need to feel that clinicians recognize their need for information and are willing to spend time answering their questions and explaining the treatment regimen.

The nurse can also assist by identifying patients or families who appear very dissatisfied with their care, particularly if the patient has had a complication resulting in injury. Families and patients who continuously criticize or question the quality of the care or the caregivers, or who appear angry, are signaling an erosion in the therapeutic relationship. Because nurses spend so much time with patients and their families, they are likely to have a solid understanding of the patient's (and the family's) psychosocial state and are often the first to recognize when they are dissatisfied. If a nurse recognizes these signs and the patient has had an adverse event, this information needs to be communicated to the health care team and the risk manager. The risk manager and all health care providers then need to meet to determine an action plan.[5]

In the past decade, nurses have made great strides in increasing their responsibilities, independence, and stature as health care professionals. But these gains have been accompanied by an increased risk of liability.[6] Claims data from the Risk Management Foundation of the Harvard Medical Institutions from 1976 to 1981 and from 1982 to 1987 reveal a 31% increase in the number of lawsuits naming a nurse or a nursing service as a defendant.[7] The expanding role of the nurse is certainly a major factor in this increase. As the nurse has evolved as a professional, legal accountability has followed.

A possible contributing factor may be the breakdown of the nurse-patient relationship, somewhat analogous to the phenomenon that occurred with physicians with the demise of the family physician and the move to specialty medicine. Nurses no longer have the opportunities to establish relationships with patients that existed in the past. Since the prospective payment system has changed the entire standard of health care, patients move through the acute care system much more quickly. And in some hospitals, the shorter in-patient stay is further fragmented by moving the patient within the hospital from one unit to another. All this leads to unfamiliarity, and a nurse who is unfamiliar with her patients may be more likely to make an error. It is clear that with no established and ongoing relationship, if a mistake does occur, lack of rapport may be part of the situation. This problem makes it even more important that nurses try their best to become as familiar as possible with patients, even on a short-term basis.

THE LEGAL PROCESS

Although the chance of actually being named in a claim is small, the fear of being sued for malpractice is pervasive among nurses and all health care providers. The undeniable emotional stress of being involved in a malpractice claim may also be exacerbated by myths and misunderstandings associated with the entire process. Dispelling those myths and clarifying the misunderstandings is essential to helping nurses and others pursue their objectives.[8] An understanding of the legal process is helpful in this regard.

When all efforts to prevent claims of malpractice have failed, the usual outcome is that the injured party (the plaintiff) pursues an action at law. In many situations, with a good risk management program in place, a private settlement will take the place of a public legal action.[9] If the plaintiff has a true injury, that is, an injury serious in nature and caused by the negligence of a health care provider, compensation should be given. There is no reason why the expense of litigation should be paid when a true claim occurs. All parties named as defendants (usually physician, hospital, and nurse, if appropriate), as well as insurance companies and attorneys, should work toward a fair settlement if a valid malpractice claim is filed.

If the plaintiff has not been satisfied by the initial efforts of the hospital and risk manager, then the next step is usually a visit to an attorney. The patient will request an interview to discuss his or her potential claim. The attorney will then, with the patient's written authorization, request a copy of the medical records.

At this point, the documentation on the medical records, especially nurses' notes, plays a vital role. Often a case is initiated because of poor documentation. Sometimes the attorney finds in the medical record evidence pointing to a different basis for claim other than the incident that the patient has described.

On one such occasion, an injured patient visited the attorney to discuss his dissatisfaction with the results of his hospitalization. During his surgical procedure, he had received a blood transfusion which he needed, but following the transfusion, he had experienced an adverse reaction. The attorney reviewed the patient's medical record. He realized that the blood was the proper type, that all policies and procedures had been properly followed, and that the policy itself had set a reasonable standard. Despite the due care exhibited by the institution, the patient had simply had a reaction—there was no negligence involved. However, the attorney noted on the record two additional factors. One was the absence of a consent form for the surgical procedure. The other was the omission of a dose of medication with the inappropriate notation "incident report filed." On the basis of these two factors, a lawsuit was initiated.[10] Had there been a valid surgical consent documented, no case would have been bought. And if the nurse who omitted the one dose of medication had not charted "incident report filed," the situation may have been quite different. One simple omission and one simple notation meant that all the time, money, and emotional energy of a lawsuit had to be undergone.

Many claims are brought to court that simply should not have been initiated. In one category, there is an obviously valid claim, and the defendant should make an honest attempt to reach a fair settlement out of court. In the second, the claim is specious: that is, there is no justification, from a legal viewpoint, for initiating an action. This is often referred to as a **nuisance claim**.

Many plaintiff's attorneys, on receipt of the medical record, will immediately forward it for review to a qualified physician or nurse to determine whether there is a medical basis for alleging a deviation from reasonable standards of care, as well as to prove causation and damages if there is. This procedure is proper, and attorneys should be encouraged to begin their evaluation of the case in this manner. In most instances, attorneys themselves do not have medical expertise to provide this initial determination. The attorney who fails to do this runs the risk of being sued for malpractice for not initiating a claim that is valid. Some law firms, particularly large malpractice firms, are now employing nurses to perform this first evaluation.

When the medical records department receives requests of this kind, the risk manager should routinely review the situation. This may be the first notice received by the hospital that a particular patient is contemplating a suit. At the very first notice of any such intention, an in-hospital investigation should take place, as well as communication with the hospital's insurance carrier. The physician involved in the case should also be notified and given an opportunity to review the record. It is vital that no changes be made in the medical record after a lawsuit is initiated. If, at this point, it is determined that the record is incomplete or inaccurate, this should be clarified in an addendum to the record with the correct date documented. It is extremely difficult to explain and define in court any change that has been made subsequent to the request for the record.

Once the attorney reviews the record and determines that the basis for the claim is appropriate and timely he or she will file a **Complaint**: a summary, in legal terms, of what the injured party is going to try to prove. This legal document is filed in the courthouse, and copies are presented to the defendants personally, along with a **Summons**. The summons notifies the defendant of the date by which an **Answer** to the complaint must be filed. In most jurisdictions, the complaint goes to a lower level judge. In jurisdictions with an arbitration system, the arbitration panel receives the complaint and initially hears the case. The case may then be appealed to the designated court.

The filing of the complaint begins the time known as the **discovery period**. The purpose of discovery is to ensure that each party has time to become fully aware of all the facts involved in the case and of the allegations of the parties regarding these facts. Another purpose is to encourage the settlement of suits when appropriate. During this time, the parties are given opportunities to gather evidence and attempt to understand the facts of the case. **Depositions**, or testimonies under oath, will be scheduled for the plaintiff, defendants, and witnesses. A court stenographer will record all depositions so that all attorneys involved have an opportunity to question the parties.

The most important type of discovery in which the nurse defendant will be required to participate in is his or her deposition. At the deposition, the nurse will provide testimony under oath which is recorded by a stenographer. The nurse defendant will be asked to respond to questions posed by the plaintiff's attorney. Other attorneys representing additional parties may also be present and have a right to ask questions. The nurse defendant's lawyer will be present to protect the nurse's rights and help him or her with the answers. Although the nurse's lawyer may ask questions, he or she will generally decline to do so. If the case is carried to trial, transcripts from the deposition may be introduced as evidence and compared with courtroom testimony for any discrepancies or contradictions.

Although the deposition process may sound innocuous, it is not. Considerable time will be spent with the lawyer preparing for it. The issues regarding depositions for defendants are also pertinent to nurses subpoenaed (served with a written notice to appear in court) to testify at depositions as fact witnesses, who will be discussing their care of the patient but not offering their opinion as an expert would. Nurses and other health care providers subpoenaed to a deposition in malpractice actions in which they are not named defendants should also be represented by counsel. Most importantly, one should never go to a deposition unprepared.

Although a deposition is a stressful experience, the nurse's lawyer will attempt to make it as pain free as possible by devoting ample time to preparing the nurse for his or her testimony to ensure that the nurse is ready to go forward and able to do the best possible job at the deposition.[11] Some attorneys will use **interrogatories**, or lists of written questions provided to the parties, to determine the evidence that is available. The plaintiff's attorney may request from the hospital all records, policies and procedures, and committee minutes pertaining to the plaintiff's case.

In many instances, these documents are protected from discovery under Peer Review Acts. These statutes, which are legislative enactments designed to encourage physicians to engage in peer review, protect such material from review by attorneys pursuing malpractice claims. Each jurisdiction will have different statutes governing what may be made available to opposing counsel.

After a malpractice suit is initiated, the nurse defendant will be required to devote considerable time and energy preparing the case, over and above the actual trial and trial preparation (90% of all malpractice cases do not reach trial). The attorney will look to the nurse for information regarding the nursing care rendered in the case and treatment issues relevant to the lawsuit. The lawyer may also ask questions that will help in selecting the proper type of expert witnesses and in developing an argument regarding the plaintiff's expert's opinion. Most of the nurse's time, however, will be devoted to preparing for and responding to certain discovery requests from the plaintiff's attorney.[12]

In many complex malpractice cases, the discovery period may last 1 or 2 years or even longer. After this period has ended, the parties will be ready to appear in court. In court, both plaintiff and defendants, was well as any witnesses, will have the opportunity to testify. Witnesses will include those persons who have knowledge of the actual incident, expert witnesses who will offer opinions about the case, and family members who may attest to the pain and suffering of the plaintiff.

In cases heard initially in a court, rather than by an arbitration panel, the case is brought before a jury composed of members of the community. Their duty in a medical malpractice case is to decide issues of fact, since in almost every malpractice case, the parties involved make contradictory statements. For example, an injured party testifies that she was injured while she was a patient at a hospital. She states that she had to go to the bathroom and called the nurse for assistance and that the nurse did not answer her call button. The nurse, however, testifies that she had responded by telling the patient not to get out of bed alone and that she would be right with her. The patient went to the bathroom alone, fell, and fractured her hip.

The jury must weigh the credibility of the two persons testifying, listen to all the other evidence, and decide which of the two parties to believe. In many instances, it is not a question of truth telling but rather of what the parties involved remember after a long period has elapsed.

The judge's role, in a malpractice case, is to monitor the testimony, to decide legal questions regarding how the evidence is presented, and to determine questions of law. After all the testimony has been presented, the judge discusses with the jury how the law should be applied. The jury decides, in most cases, whether negligence has occurred and what damages should be awarded. It should be remembered that, at any point before the jury's decision, the parties themselves may decide to settle the case and remove it from the jury's province. Settlements do not usually receive the publicity that large jury verdicts produce. In fact, one stipulation of a settlement may be that the contents are confidential.[13]

Nurses who are named as defendants in malpractice lawsuits are unlikely to be comforted by statistics indicating that, overall, the incidence of nurses being sued is low. However, a nurse who has just been named as a defendant in a malpractice lawsuit should not panic or fear that his or her nursing career is over.

Being sued for the care and treatment rendered to a patient, regardless of the merits of the allegations, will most likely be a difficult and painful experience for any nurse. With the guidance and assistance of a good malpractice defense lawyer, insurance claim representative, and risk manager, nurses who are named in malpractice claims should experience little disruption in their professional and personal lives. In addition, the nurse defendant will probably find his or her colleagues to be supportive and nonjudgmental. Nurses know that being sued for malpractice is an inherent risk of nursing and that being named in a claim is not necessarily a reflection of one's standards of practice or abilities.[14]

NOTES

1. Craddick, Joyce W. (1986). Medical management analysis in 1986, In Chapman-Cliburn (Ed.), *Issues and Interactions at 72.* Vanagunas, Audrey M. & Halleen, Natalie. (1986, January–March). Chicago hospital risk pooling program completes study of concurrent monitoring. 1 Occurrence 1-4

2. Pennsylvania Hospital Insurance Company (PHICO). (1978).

3. Greenlaw, J. (1982, September). Documentation of patient care: An often underestimated responsibility. *Law, Medicine and Health Care, 10* (4) 172.

4. Roach, W. (1985). Medical records and the law. (MD: Aspen Publications).

5. Reiley, Peg and Kirle, Leslie. (1993, March). Risk management in the practice of nursing, *Forum*, 9.

6. No author listed (1992, February). Preventing nursing liability. *Hospital Risk Control Update.* ECRI.

7. Morlock, L.L. and Malitz, F.E. (1991, Spring). Do hospital risk management programs make a difference? Relationships between risk management program activities and hospital malpractice claims experience. *Law and Contemporary Problems, 54* (2), 1-22.

8. Dasse, Priscilla S., Editor (1993, March). Editor's Note. *Forum.*

9. Fiesta, Janine (1988). *The Law and Liability: A Guide for Nurses* (2nd ed.), (New York: Wiley).

10. Troyer, Glenn, & Salmon, Steven L. (1986). Handbook of health care risk management. (MD: Aspen Publications).

11. Nelson, Kim (1993, March). The nurse as a malpractice defendant. *Forum*, 13.

12. Ibid.

13. Fiesta, Janine. (1991). Legal procedures. *Nursing Management, 22* (7), 12–13.

14. Nelson, Kim. (1993, March). The nurse as a malpractice defendant, *Forum*, 12.

Chapter 18

Making a Malpractice Case Worse

Making a bad situation worse is a major pitfall and occurs all too frequently. There are any number of ways to make a malpractice case worse. They include lying and practicing fraud, behaving in a grossly negligent way, and acting with malice.

FRAUD

The paramount way to make a case worse is to practice in a fraudulent or dishonest manner—in other words, to commit an act of malpractice and then attempt to cover it up. Honesty is still always the best policy. Alteration of hospital records is one example of an attempt to cover up an event.

In *Hiatt v. Grace*,[1] the nurse's failure to notify a physician that delivery was imminent caused the patient's delivery to be unattended by a physician. As a result, the woman sustained lacerations that caused a loss of sensation in the vagina and labia. Among other allegations, the lawsuit alleged abandonment, which is defined as the unilateral severance of the professional relationship with the patient without adequate notice and while the necessity for care still exists. The mother and father of the patient testified that they repeatedly called the nurse and reported their observations of pain and severe contractions.

The patient's husband testified that he told the nurse of the patient's complaints of increased pain. He also told the nurses that during the patient's first labor, delivery progressed rapidly after the patient was dilated 8 cm. The nurse allegedly told him not to worry and kept reading a magazine. Shortly thereafter, the nurse checked on the patient and told her she was 8 cm dilated. The husband repeatedly requested that the nurse notify the physician, but she refused to do so.

At trial, the obstetrician testified that he expected the nurse to take into consideration various factors and to exercise independent judgment as to notifying him about the impending delivery. Expert witness testimony by an obstetrical nursing instructor established that the nurse's care fell below the standard of care of the nursing profession in the nurse's community. The evidence also showed that the hospital records had been altered to show that the physician delivered the patient's baby when in fact the nurse did so.

In another case, a nurse patient sued an ophthalmologist, claiming that never during the course of treatment had the defendant recommended hospitalization and biopsy even though she had asked about a biopsy. Her eye was removed and radial neck dissection was performed. The plaintiff's attorney indicated that records may have been altered: notations indicating that the patient refused to be hospitalized and have a biopsy appeared to be written in a lighter ink than the rest of the entries. Further, the attorney argued that the physician would have "had patient sign something if she was so vehement about refusing advice." The case settled for $550,000.[2]

Lying in court is another obvious way to make a case worse. In an interesting nursing home case, the plaintiff's decedent, a 75-year-old nursing home patient, was allegedly given a placebo instead of the drug morphine for his pain therapy. He was suffering from intractable pain due to cancer. The plaintiff also alleged that drugs other than morphine were administered to the decedent and that the defendants, in effect, experimented with treating the pain. The defendants insisted that they followed the physician's orders, that they gave drugs when the decedent asked for them, and that they gave no placebos. However, the plaintiff's niece had intercepted a letter stating that a placebo was given: "We tried a liquid juice with no medication in it." A $15 million verdict, consisting of $7.5 million in punitive damages, was returned.[3]

In a New Jersey case, allegations included missing risk management reports, fetal monitor strips, and contract with an outside laboratory. The case involved failure to diagnose labor and to diagnose an emergency cesarean section, a failure which caused brain damage, cerebral palsy, and seizure disorder. The defendants claimed the standard of care allowed them to wait until a lung maturity test was returned before performing an emergency cesarean section, and that it took between 24 and 48 hours for the test to be returned from an outside lab. However, the plaintiff's counsel unearthed evidence that the test could be returned in 6 hours. The defendants were also accused of lying in depositions and interrogatories. A settlement of $1.3 million was reached.[4]

A more recent variety of fraud has been the examples of false testimony by expert witnesses in malpractice cases. One physician testified falsely that he was board-certified in thoracic surgery. His curriculum vitae also had other false information. He was charged with immoral conduct and making false records in the practice of medicine.[5]

PUNITIVE DAMAGES

An altered medical record or for that matter any form of fraud may result in a **punitive damage** award. Punitive damages are damages awarded to a plaintiff in a lawsuit over and above ordinary damages.

They are intended to solace the plaintiff for mental anguish, laceration of his or her feelings, or else to punish the defendant for his evil behavior or to make an example of him.[6]

The focus of punitive damage is on the conduct of the particular defendant. The issue often arises of whether the defendant's conduct supports an award of punitive damages and whether there is sufficient evidence to present the question to the jury. In *Adams v. Murakami*,[7] a mentally ill patient was impregnated by another patient during hospitalization. The plaintiff gave birth to a son who was later diagnosed as mentally retarded and autistic. After a jury trial, a verdict was returned for the plaintiff on claims of medical malpractice and intentional infliction of emotional distress. After adjustments by the trial court, the award totaled $1,024,266, including $750,000 in punitive damages. On appeal, the defendant contended that the punitive damage award should be set aside. The court noted that the purpose of punitive damage awards is to punish wrongdoing and deter similar future misconduct. The California Supreme Court ultimately overturned the award because of insufficient evidence.

Punitive damage awards are relatively rare in malpractice cases.[8] In order to warrant such an award, the act must not only be willful or intentional but, in most cases, must also be accompanied by aggravating circumstances that amount to gross negligence or, in some cases, malice. Theoretically, the defendants in a malpractice action, usually health care professionals, are motivated by a desire to heal people, and their conduct is seldom sufficiently egregious to give rise to a claim for punitive damages, even where there are grave errors in judgment or practice. Nonetheless, there are cases where extenuating circumstances such as misrepresentation, battery, and gross negligence have served as a basis for a punitive damage claim.

GROSS NEGLIGENCE

To establish gross negligence, there must be evidence which makes it fair to conclude that the defendant had decided to ignore the rights of the injured party, even in light of the probable and threatened injury. Gross negligence is frequently characterized by conscious indifference to the rights, welfare, and safety of others and can be inferred from all acts, omissions, and circumstances. Conscious indifference "denotes a decision, in the face of an impending harm to another party, to not care about the consequences of the act which may ultimately lead to that harm."

In a Texas case, a hospital was found guilty of gross negligence. A 33-year-old woman was brought to Texarkana Memorial Hospital d/b/a Wadley Regional Medical Center. She was admitted by the emergency room physician, whose initial assessment was that she had been nervous and upset for 2 months, was depressed and possibly suicidal, was unable to sleep, and was hallucinating. The patient was given medication, and the doctor, the hospital's staff physician for psychiatry, was called. The doctor determined that the patient was psychotic and requested that she be placed in the hospital's closed unit. He gave routine orders for laboratory work and prescribed a major tranquilizer. On two occasions, the patient threatened to jump out of the hospital room window. She told the nurse on duty that she felt someone was trying to kill her. She put on her clothes and attempted to leave the hospital. The doctor then ordered the dosage of the patient's medication to be increased. At about 6:00 p.m. the nurse on duty in the open unit requested additional help because of the situation. The hospital supervisor on duty at first refused to send any additional help. A nurse informed him, "I have a patient who wants to jump out a window, seriously." He then replied that he would see what he could do. At about 7:10 p.m. the supervisor "floated" a registered nurse to the open unit as additional help. The nurse advised that the patient needed someone with her constantly. At approximately 11:00 p.m. the registered nurse called the hospital administrator and advised that the patient was asleep. She was granted permission to go home, no replacement was assigned, and the patient jumped from her hospital room window to her death.

A jury awarded substantial actual and exemplary damages of nearly $1 million to the decedent's administratrix. The hospital appealed. The Court of Appeals of Texas affirmed the judgment of the lower court and held that the evidence was sufficient to establish gross negligence on behalf of the hospital. The court noted that a plaintiff is not required to produce direct evidence of the defendant's objective state of mind, but that his mental state may be inferred when the evidence demonstrates that under all circumstances, a reasonable, prudent person would have realized that his or her conduct created an extreme degree of risk to the safety of others.[9]

In *Clay v. National Health Care*, the plaintiff, a 69-year-old retired salesman, had knee surgery at Lakeside Community Hospital in January 1987. The only anesthesiologist at the hospital prematurely extubated the plaintiff in the recovery room while he was still under the effect of the anesthesia. His condition deteriorated. The recovery room nurse noted the deterioration and called the anesthesiologist, but the anesthesiologist failed to give the appropriate care. The recovery room nurse did not call another doctor or attempt to ventilate him until after he suffered an arrest. A code was called and the plaintiff was resuscitated, but he had suffered brain damage affecting motor function and spatial perception, which causes difficulty in walking. The plaintiff contended that the hospital was liable for the doctor's negligence and for the nurses' negligence and that the hospital was also liable for allowing her to continue to provide anesthesia despite numerous complaints from the hospital's nursing staff and her complaints to the hospital administrator that she was overworked and needed additional assistance. She contended that she acted properly when extubation occurred and that the recovery room nurse failed to give her appropriate information to respond appropriately to treat the plaintiff. The hospital denied negligence by the nurses and also denied that the doctor was its agent. It also claimed that it did not have sufficient information to relieve Dr. Miller from her duties. The jury awarded the plaintiff and his wife $12 million each in punitive damages.[10]

MALICE

Malice is defined as knowing that a statement is false or making the statement with reckless disregard of whether it is true or not or acting in malice.[11] In general an award of punitive damages requires evidence of malice rather than simply negligent conduct. The Maryland high court ruled that a jury may award a patient punitive damages for a hospital's failure to disclose her medical records, even without any evidence that the hospital acted maliciously in not acceding to the patient's request. A couple sued a hospital for damages, claiming that the hospital had failed to comply with their request to obtain copies of medical records relating to the wife's hospitalization for the birth of a child. A jury awarded the couple $300,000 in actual damages and $700,000 in punitive damages. The hospital appealed, arguing that the punitive damages award was invalid under Maryland law because there had been no evidence that the hospital had acted with malice.[12] The state supreme court disagreed and upheld the award, emphasizing that the law simply states that a hospital is liable for punitive damages if it does not disclose a medical record as required. Nowhere in the statute, the court asserted, is there any indication that the legislature intended that proof of actual or implied malice be a prerequisite to liability for punitive damages. The purpose of the statute is to compel disclosure of medical records under specific circumstances and to attain uniformity by having all facilities bound by the same rules.

Therefore, the court concluded, the jury's award was proper because the mere refusal to disclose a record within a reasonable time following a request is sufficient to generate liability for punitive damages.

MISREPRESENTATION

Misrepresentation of facts to a patient, which includes omitting important facts, is another serious offense. In one case, when a Veteran's Administration hospital failed to tell a nurse employee about abnormalities that appeared on x-rays taken during employment examinations, the jury awarded almost $500,000. As part of a preemployment physical examination, the nurse had a chest x-ray and a tuberculosis test and was not informed of these tests' abnormal findings.[13]

Misrepresentation was also a part of the case against Dr. Burt, who claimed that his surgical procedures caused women to become "horny little mice."[14] These claims were made in his 1975 book *The Surgery of Love*. In fact, these procedures, including female circumcision and realignment of the vagina, left women unable to have sex or urinate properly, in chronic pain with constant infections, and in emotional distress. According to some, the surgery was performed without their consent during an episiotomy after childbirth. A number of these cases are currently in litigation.

In a recent study, among factors cited as reasons for filing lawsuits was the perception that patients and families had been misled.[15]

EMOTIONAL DISTRESS

The allegation of emotional distress is sometimes part of a serious malpractice case. In one instance a hospital had to pay $500,000 to a Jehovah Witness patient. The hospital convinced the patient to undergo surgery by stating it was willing to perform a kidney transplant without authorization to administer transfusions, when in fact the hospital had arranged to get a court order for transfusions. The parents of the patient had begun making arrangements to have surgery performed at another facility when the hospital made these assurances. Although no transfusions were needed during surgery, the hospital administered a transfusion after the procedure when the patient's heart rate rose and blood pressure dropped. The intentional infliction of emotional distress was alleged.[16]

Traditionally, to prove emotional distress one had to show an accompanying physical impact and physical symptoms. In cases where a third party "bystander"—such as a family member observing the patients' distress—sued for their own emotional harm, the absence of physical injury precluded the lawsuit. Recent decisions suggest, however, that there may be an emerging trend favoring expanded liability to third parties who experience emotional distress as a result of an act of malpractice directed at a patient.[17] One of the leading cases is *Molien v. Kaiser Foundation Hospitals*.[18] The complaint alleged that the patient went to Kaiser for a routine physical examination and that a staff physician negligently examined and tested her, and erroneously advised her that she had contracted syphylis. The defendant instructed her to advise her husband of the diagnosis. The husband (the plaintiff) underwent blood tests to determine whether he had the disease, and the test results were negative; nonetheless, as a result of the misdiagnosis, the plaintiff's wife became suspicious that he had engaged in extramarital sexual activities. This eventually resulted in a breakup of their marriage, causing the plaintiff to suffer extreme emotional distress as a result of the defendant's negligence.

The purpose of punitive damages is to deter repetition of reprehensible conduct.[19] Punitive damages are damages awarded over and above compensation. Punitive damages may solace the patient for emotional anguish, punish the defendant for intentional conduct or make an example of him or her.[20]

In one case a baby was stillborn, and shortly after the fetus was delivered, hospital employees mailed the plaintiff a birth certificate and a card proclaiming "It's a boy!" The documents bore the footprints and listed the height and weight of the fetus, which physicians determined to have died sometime before birth. The plaintiff contended that the hospital employees acted in an outrageous manner and that they intentionally sought to inflict emotional distress. The plaintiff sought punitive damages for emotional distress. The defendant contended that the hospital staff simply followed established practice in trying to ease the parent's grief over the loss of a child. The defendant filed a motion for summary judgment, which was granted, and the case was dismissed.[21]

In a Pennsylvania case, the patient claimed the negligent infliction of emotional distress based upon her hearing loud and vulgar language from hospital employees watching a male stripper in the next room while she was waiting for an x-ray examination. A verdict for the defendant was returned by the jury.[22]

Sometimes emotional distress is hard to establish, and verdicts may be unpredictable. In a Tennessee case, the patient was admitted for a hysterectomy. The nurse allegedly stood behind the patient's husband, put her arms around him, laid her cheek on his back, and laughed. The patient believed the nurse was laughing at her and saying she could take her husband away because of her condition. The court held that this was not outrageous behavior "because there was no evidence as to the standard of civilized society within the hospital environment". The court stated that an ordinary reasonable person would not think this kind of conduct would cause an injury.[23] However, a Louisiana court has allowed a claim for emotional distress brought by a woman whose husband allegedly sustained numerous rat bites during a hospital stay.[24]

In a case alleging improper autopsy experimentation, a pathologist dropped a deceased infant's body headfirst to concrete causing a skull fracture. He was conducting this "experiment" because he was testifying that another father had not intentionally killed his son, but accidentally dropped him. The plaintiff is seeking $2 million for emotional suffering. The doctor was also charged with falsifying the autopsy report, which did not mention skull fracture. Research was not needed to determine the cause of his death.[25]

In another case, a 3-day-old infant was dropped 4 feet on his head by a nurse and suffered brain damage. The court awarded $1.2 million for the child and $500,000 for the mother's mental anguish. The intensive care nurse testified that an intravenous tube wrapped around infant's leg became caught on the incubator's door, and when the nurse opened the door to remove baby, he was thrown to the ground.[26]

THE IMPORTANCE OF ATTITUDE

A negative attitude is a significant factor in not only prompting clients to initiate a malpractice claim, as shown in previous chapters, but also in making a case worse. It is important for the nurse to cooperate with the defense attorney. Unfortunately, sometimes the nurse is hostile or arrogant. This impinges upon the attorneys ability to defend the case as fully as possible; communication is inhibited. If this attitude is also conveyed to the jury, a negative response may occur. Sometimes defensible malpractice cases are settled because defense counsel fears the effect of the witness's personality or attitude upon the jury's ability to assess the case objectively.

NOTES

1. Hiatt v. Grace, 523 P. 2d 320 (Kans. 1974)

2. Memmoli v. Broderick, 946 F 2d 1467 (Md. 1992).

3. Falson, Adminx. of the Estate of Henry James v. The Hillhaven Corp. d/b/a Guardian Care of Ahoskie and Rebecca Carter, No. 89CVS64. (1991). *Medical Malpractice Verdicts, Settlements & Experts, 7* (3), 35.

4. Kelly v. New Jersey University of Medicine and Dentistry Hospital et al., No. UNN-L-03532-89. (1992, October) *Medical Malpractice Verdicts, Settlements & Experts, 8* (10), 32–33.

5. Joseph v. Board of Medicine, 587 A.2d 1085 (D.C. App. 1991).

6. Horty, John, Editor (1987, December/1988, January). Nursing standard of care increasing, *Patient Care Law,* An Action-Kit Publication, 1.

7. Adams v. Murahami, 284 Calif. Rptr. 318, 813 P.2d 1348 (1991).

8. Nelson, L., Editor (1992). Punitive damages in malpractice cases. *Medical Malpractice 5* (6), 82-86.

9. Texarkana Memorial Hospital, Inc. v. Firth, 746 S.W.2d 949 (Tex. 1988).

10. Clay v. National Health Care, No. 89-18326. (1991). *Medical Malpractice Verdicts, Settlements & Experts, 7* (1), 1.

11. Stickler, Bruce and Mark Nelson, (May 1988). Defamation in the Workplace: Employer Rights and Responsibilities. *Journal of Hospital and Health Law, 21* (5), 97.

12. Franklin Square Hospital v. Laubach, 569 A.2d 693 (Md. l990).

13. Daly v. U.S., 946 F.2d 1467 (Wash., 1991)

14. (1989, February 6). Bar Talk. *Pennsylvania Law Journal Reporter*, 3.

15. Hickson, Gerald B., M.D.; et al. (1992). Factors that prompted families to file medical malpractice claims following perinatal injuries. *Journal of the American Medical Association, 267* (10), 1359–63.

16. Lunsford v. Regents of University of California. (1990, September). *Hospital Law Manual,* 125, 14.

17. Nelson, Leonard, Editor (1989). Liability of health care providers to third parties for negligent infliction of emotional distress. *Medical Malpractice Reports, 2* (6), 82–86.

18. Molien v. Kaiser Foundation Hospitals, 27 Calif. 3d 916, 167 Calif. Rptr. 831, 616 P.2d 813 (1980).

19. Springer. Punitive Damages, *Patient Care Law.*, Action-Kit, (JAN 88).

20. Gwinnett County v. Jones, 409 S.E. 2d 501 (Ga. 1991).

21. Janice F. Wilson v. HCA Southern Hills Medical Center, Davidson County (TN) Cir. Ct. No. 91C-3436. (1992). *Medical Malpractice Verdicts, Settlements & Experts, 8* (10), 25.

22. Abadie v. Riddle Memorial Hospital, 589 A.2d 1143 (1991).

23. Highfill v. Baptist Hospital, 819 S.E. 436 (Tenn. 1991).

24. LeJeune v. Rayne Branch Hospital, 539 S.E.2d 849 (La. 1990).

25. Arnaud v. Odom, Thompson, MD and Louisiana State University School of Medicine, No. 87-7849. (1992, July).

26. Bond v. Sacred Heart Medical Center, No. 86-2-03311-9. (1991, October) *Medical Malpractice Verdicts, Settlements & Experts, 7* (10), 33.

Chapter 19

Not Following Documentation Principles

As has been said many times in previous chapters, careful documentation is one of the main defenses against liability exposure. Documentation should be thorough and accurate without being excessive. Achieving this balance is not easy and is one of the continuing challenges in nursing.

THE IMPORTANCE OF NURSES' NOTES

Nurses' notes are important documents: they literally and figuratively stand out like a red flag.[1] Physicians are required to read these notes and can be held liable if they do not. In a Kansas case, the patient had bypass surgery and had problems with the leg incision. It did not seem to be healing properly, so she mentioned this to the nurse. The nurse indicated some "bloody oozing from the incision." The patient continued to have problems, and about a year later an x-ray revealed that hemoclips had been left in the leg. Because an expert witness was not produced, the claim was dismissed.[2] It appears that if the plaintiff had provided the necessary expert medical testimony, both the hospital and the doctor would be hard-pressed to explain why no one, particularly the attending physician, paid heed to the patient's complaint or the nurse's notes.

Furthermore, physicians are not permitted to amend nurses' notes. In *Henry v. St. John's Hospital*, the nursing notes indicated that the patient, while in labor, had been given 6 cc of Marcaine on each side by the resident physician. The baby experienced fetal distress, and the physician then amended the notes to show a lesser dosage.[3] The jury awarded $10 million. The resident physician's conduct in amending the nursing notes was not only morally reprehensible but trampled the most basic and fundamental standards and principles between responsible nursing personnel and responsible physicians. Such an action should be the subject of outrage by the nursing department.[4]

Inappropriate comments in the chart are another source of documentation difficulty in legal cases. In one case, an elderly hospital patient had developed bedsores, and her family complained that she wasn't getting proper care. When she died of unknown but probably natural causes, the family sued. In her chart, under "prognosis," the physician had written "PBBB." After learning that this stood for "pine box by bedside," the insurance company decided to settle for $38,000.[5]

BEING ACCURATE AND THOROUGH

Unfortunately, there are many pitfalls associated with charting, and what the nurse documents can sometimes be an issue in malpractice cases. In *Surratt v. Prince George's County* (1990)[6], the plaintiffs alleged that antenatal fetal monitoring strips were misinterpreted as reassuring when they were ominous and should have been followed with further testing which would have led to earlier delivery of the child. The baby was born severely depressed and died 14 days later. A key issue in the case was a nurse's handwritten note "audible decel heart" on a portion of the fetal monitor tracing which actually was unreadable artifact. The defense expert testified that it was impossible for the ear to hear a valid signal if the tracing recorded only artifact. At trial, the plaintiffs presented a pregnant woman on a gurney hooked to a fetal monitor and had their expert thump on her abdomen to cause a paper artifact while the jury was still able to hear the fetal heart. The jury awarded over $500,000, but the judge reduced the amount by almost $200,000.

To avoid liability, it is important to be accurate and thorough. For example, erroneous charting may be a problem in a malpractice case. In one instance an erroneous entry in the medical records stating that the patient had undergone an appendectomy may have led to a failure to diagnose appendicitis. The delay in treatment led to a $30,000 verdict.[7] In *Long v. St. Vincent's Hospital*, the patient had pain and limited mobility following an injection in the left hip. The nurse stated at her deposition that she administered the injection in the right hip, but at trial stated left hip in conformity with the chart. The jury returned a $250,000 verdict.[8]

In another case, a Kentucky hospital was liable with the attending physician for the death of a patient from brain damage which resulted from untreated water intoxication brought on by the administration of more fluid than her body could handle.[9] At trial it was revealed that the patient's input/output records for fluids were not accurately compiled.[10] And in a Kansas case, a hospital was held liable for the failure of a nurse to fill out the "History" section of the patient's admission records, which would have revealed that the patient was in too weak a condition to be left alone on the x-ray table during an examination. When the table was rotated to a vertical position, she fell off and was injured.[11]

Proper record keeping includes being able to retrieve and use data from records of a patient's previous admissions.[12] In a Mississippi case, a

70-year-old patient was placed in the intensive care unit. At approximately 10 P.M., the nurse who had just come on shift observed that the patient's blood pressure was elevated, she was confused, her speech was unintelligible, and she had an abnormal heart rhythm. The nurse notified the physician, who, without assessing the patient, told the nurse to continue present treatment. The next morning the patient had a grand mal seizure and became comatose. A computerized axial tomography scan indicated a subarachnoid aneurysm which had hemorrhaged, and 10 days later the aneurysm ruptured and the patient died. A jury verdict in favor of the defendants was reached, and the plaintiffs appealed. The Supreme Court of Mississippi reversed the case and held that the trial court had committed error in failing to place the burden on the hospital to show that the medical chart was not lost or destroyed by the hospital. The hospital had presented a "reconstructed medical record." The evidence indicated that the director of nurses had instructed the records custodian to "lock up" the records. However, it was discovered that the chart was missing and the reconstructed version was made. The court found that the jury was entitled to be told that the original hospital record would not be produced in court and that the hospital had the duty to give an adequate explanation for the absence of the original hospital records. The explanation for the absence of the original might be satisfactory if it could be shown that the record was lost through no fault of the hospital.[13]

It is important to be thorough as well as accurate. In one case, failure to record critical information about a patient in his chart was found to be actionable under the Texas Tort Claims Act.[14] The patient was injured in an accident which left him partially paralyzed and functionally impaired due to severe brain damage. He was admitted for an intensive rehabilitation program, and shortly after arriving at the hospital, he broke his right hip. His parents reported a missing support from the right side of the wheelchair as well as scratches on his right arm, but the nurse failed to record these observations in the chart. His hip became red and swollen and increasingly more painful and sensitive. The mother asked the nurses to record these observations, but they did not. The court found the hospital negligent in its keeping of files, records, and other documents and awarded $250,000, which was the maximum allowed for a governmental entity to be liable under the Texas law.

Although physicians are responsible for reading nurses' notes, nurses may be responsible for both documenting and communicating orally if the nursing assessment indicates information of a serious and critical nature requiring immediate intervention. This raises another pitfall: nurses often fail to document significant information provided to the physician. The nurses' note that begins with the words "doctor notified" is frequently noted in malpractice cases because of the absence of what specific information was provided to the physician.

In general, the omission of significant information is a major problem in nursing notes. The failure to document discharge instructions has been a recently identified issue. In this case, because hospital emergency department personnel provided an "After-Care Instruction Sheet," the court held that the parents had received appropriate instructions to return with their child, who was subsequently diagnosed with meningitis.[15] The presence of this instruction sheet led to a verdict for the defense.

A WORD OF CAUTION

Having said all this, however, it is also crucial to remember that nurses cannot be expected to function as court stenographers as they practice their profession. It is most unrealistic to expect the nurse to write every single action or word exchanged with the patient, family, and physician and yet provide the necessary bedside care, patient management, and health teaching which are the substance of the nurse's professional responsibility.

If this concept is not understood and nurses become obsessed with the dictum "If it wasn't charted, it wasn't done," they can be their own worst enemies. By perpetuating the incorrect presumption that nurses must chart "everything that is done for the patient," individual nurses have done the nursing profession a great disservice in court, especially when the nurse is an expert witness in a malpractice case and memorializes the above statement in testimony. In doing this the nurse not only affects the outcome of the particular case but perhaps, more importantly, reinforces for the judge, jury, attorneys, media, and others that this concept can be generalized and applied to all situations. When this happens, the absence of documentation may lead to a negative outcome in a malpractice case when, in fact, no negligence has occurred. Remember, even if an act was not charted, it *may have been done.*

In *Jarvis v. St. Charles Medical Center*[16], the patient was admitted with a fractured leg, and her physician became concerned about the possible development of compartment syndrome. He left instructions with the nurses to perform tests and observations on an hourly basis and to notify him if problems developed, When examining the patient 2 days later, the physician observed that her foot was white and that there was no discernible pulse. The nurses' notes recorded sporadic testing. The court held that there was a reasonable probability that the change in the condition of the leg became discernible several hours before the physician saw the patient. A 0400 note indicated no change in circulation, movement, or sensation. When the physician examined the patient at 0830, her foot was white and there was no pulse. Surgery was performed immediately, but the patient has restricted use of her leg.

Because this patient had shown some symptoms of compartment syndrome, which seemed to be alleviated after the physician spread the cast, experts for the hospital argued that the muscle death was a gradual process and that the physician did not appropriately manage the patient. The doctor defendant's theory was that a sudden change had occurred, of which the nurses should have notified him. The jury believed that the physician was negligent but that the nurses' failure to conduct the examinations was also contributory. The patient also testi-fied that the doctor had told her, "The hospital staff should have monitored you more closely." Arguably, the nurses may have checked the patient appropriately but may have neglected to chart. There is no evidence in the testimony to suggest this, but in many malpractice cases where there is an absence of documentation, such testimony does exist. And sometimes the jury believes that the nurse did act but did not chart. If the jury is not presented with the chant "If it wasn't charted, it wasn't done," it is at least conceivable that they may under-stand that nurses sometimes fail to write because they are involved in taking care of patients.

The Jarvis case also illustrates the syndrome, mentioned earlier in this book, of a health care provider blaming another for an adverse outcome to a patient. This syndrome is so pervasive that it has received its own descriptive terminology—*jousting*. At the heart of many patient visits to attorneys is a comment that has been made to the patient or family criticizing care provided by someone else. In fact, in a recent study of factors that prompted families to file medical malpractice claims following perinatal injuries,[17] over one-third of all families indicated that they were told by medical personnel prior to filing that the care provided had caused their children's injuries.

Like failure to record information, failure to produce documents may also be viewed by the jury as a purposeful attempt to conceal what actually occurred. Unfortunately, often the records are really lost or misplaced. However, exceptions do occur. In *Laubach v. Franklin*

Square Hospital (1989), the jury found that the hospital had knowingly hid the fetal heart tracings and awarded $1 million. The plaintiff claimed that the doctor was late in arriving and that the fetal heart monitor was malfunctioning and had to be replaced. The brain-damaged baby died 5 months after her birth. Failure to produce the records was in violation of a state law which provided a specific right of recovery of compensatory and punitive damages against hospitals that hide or refuse to produce records.[18]

In some case, the jury has not accepted the plaintiff's allegation of altered records. In a California case, the parents alleged that their child's severe mental retardation was due to brain hypoxia resulting from a delay in performing the caesarean section. They contended that the baby should have been delivered sooner because of earlier signs of placental insufficiency from an amniotomy on the day of delivery and from a fetal monitor strip. They further alleged that the hospital's records were erroneous and/or falsified, and that the time between the defendant doctor's decision to do the section and the actual delivery was 20 to 30 minutes or more. But the defendants contended that there were no indications for an earlier section, and that the interval between the doctor's decision to do the section and actual delivery was only 6 to 10 minutes. The jury found for the defense.[19]

DOCUMENTATION SUGGESTIONS

Since the failure to document appropriately is obviously a pivotal issue in many malpractice cases, it is important to know how much is enough and what needs to be charted. Establishing a national standard for charting may be the solution. With such a standard, a nurse would not have to learn a new system of charting in every change of work environment. A standardized medical record could be used in every hospital, as well as a standardized emergency department record, an operating room record, a home care record, and so on. Such records would not only improve communication and patient care but would also be a very effective cost control mechanism. *Nurses should move toward one national standard for charting and one form.*

The basic principles of charting are relatively simple. By definition, the purpose of the medical record is to document the medical care administered to the patient. Therefore, any information that is clinically significant should be included in the patient's medical record.

For example, sometimes the nurse forgets to document an element of clinical significance for patient care. When this happens, it is appropriate for the nurse to include this information in the chart even though it may be added at a later point. Additions that are contemporaneous with the care of the patient or even added shortly afterward are not a problem in the courtroom. Juries understand that nurses are human beings who sometimes forget to document, and they are not immune to the argument that charting is secondary to patient care. As long as the additional material is dated accurately, it is not a problem. If an item meets the definition of having clinical significance, it would be improper not to add it to the medical record for completion.

The medical record also functions as a vehicle for communication among all health care providers involved with the patient. Therefore, any item of information about the patient that meets this criterion should be documented. An example would be some fact identified by a social worker through some communication with the patient and family. In some institutions certain categories of health care workers are not permitted to chart. This presents a problem because either important material is omitted from the record or one person is asked to document the observations of another. For example, nursing assistants commonly are not permitted to document the basic nursing care they provided.

Since documentation should be comprehensive and factual, any method of charting that facilitates meeting these objectives is acceptable. Graphs, logs, checklists, and any other form of "abbreviated" charting are appropriate. Long, narrative paragraphs should be a necessary part of charting only infrequently and in exceptional circumstances. Any format for charting that allows the nurse to spend less time writing, yet meets the goals noted above, should be encouraged.

Again, although the medical record is frequently defined as a "legal document," this is actually its least important function. Certainly the medical record will be used in the courtroom if a lawsuit is initiated; however, the numbers of medical records actually involved in litigation are quite small compared with the number of medical records the nurse deals with on a daily basis. The most important aspect of the medical record is that it is meant to reflect the medical care given to the patient.

This means that charting by exception is a reasonable method of charting as long as the nursing policy defines what *charting by exception* means. Charting by exception refers to charting only the deviation rather than the norm. For example, nurses routinely observe the patients' skin condition if the patient is confined to bed. With a charting by exception system, it will be presumed that their observations are occurring and that the skin condition is normal, unless the nurse documents otherwise.[20] The documentation policy should clearly indicate that the presumption is in favor of the nurse. If it was not charted, it was done.[21]

NOTES

1. Tammelleo, A. David (1988), *The Regan Report on Nursing Law, 29* (1).

2. St. Francis Regional Medical Center v. Hale, 752 P.2d 129 (Kans. 1988).

3. Henry v. St. John's Hospital, 512 N.E.2d 1044 (Ill. 1987).

4. Tammelleo, A. David (1987). Can doctors amend nurses' notes? *The Regan Report on Nursing Law, 28* (6), 1.

5. Mangels, Linda (1990 November 12). Chart notes from a malpractice insurer's hell. *Medical Economics.*

6. Surratt v. Prince George's County (Maryland). (1990). *Medical Malpractice Verdicts, Settlements & Experts, 6* (11), 31.

7. Vargas v. Sierra Medical Group, Visalia Community Hospital (California), No. 132628. (1993). *Medical Malpractice Verdicts, Settlements & Experts, 9* (2), 13.

8. Long v. St. Vincent's Hospital (Alabama), CV-86-6832. (1990). *Medical Malpractice Verdicts, Settlements & Experts, 6* (5).

9. Rogers v. Kasdan, 612 S.W.2d 133 (Ky. 1981).

10. Smith v. St. Therese Hospital, 106 Ill. App. 3d 268, 62 Ill., Dec. 141, 435 N.E.2d 939 (1982).

11. McNight v. St. Francis Hospital & School of Nursing, 224 Kan. 632, 585 P.2d 984 (1978).

12. Rogers v. Baptist General Convention, 651 P.2d 672 (Okla. 1982).

13. DeLaughter v. Lawrence County Hospital, 601 So. 2d 818 (Miss. 1992)

14. University of Texas Medical Branch at Galveston v. York, 808 S.W.3d 106 (Tex. 1991).

15. Roberts v. Sisters of Saint Francis, 556 N.E.2d 662 (Ill. 1990).

16. Jarvis v. St. Charles Medical Center, 713 P.2d 620 (Oreg. 1986).

17. Hickson, Gerald B. et al. (March 11, 1992). The Factors that Prompted Families to File Medical Malpractice Claims Following Perinatal Injuries, *Journal of American Medical Association* 267.

18. Laubach v. Franklin Square Hospital (Maryland), No. 85248043/c139548. (1989). *Medical Malpractice Verdicts, Settlements & Experts, 5* (11), 26.

19. Pacini v. Marin Hospital (California), No. 119625. (1990). *Medical Malpractice Verdicts, Settlements & Experts, 6* (12), 38-39.

20. Burke, Laura and Murphy, Judy. *Charting by Exception Applications.* NY: Delmar, 1993

21. Ibid.

Chapter 20

Confusing Legal and Ethical Questions

Nurses, as a professional group, have had a long history of high ethical standards. They want to know what they "ought" to do, not solely what they "must" do. From the legal standpoint nurses are concerned about what they need to do to protect themselves in a litigation situation. The legal standard may be only a minimal standard; what a reasonable professional would do in a particular set of circumstances is not the highest standard of care. The ethical standard is not based upon the reasonable person but rather upon individual values as developed both personally and professionally.

Nurses often feel they are accountable for everything that goes wrong with their patients. Therefore, it is important to understand the limits of legal accountability versus ethical obligations.

INDIVIDUAL ACCOUNTABILITY

Of paramount importance is the legal principle of **primary** or **individual accountability**. This refers to the well-established fact that, as individuals, we are first and foremost accountable for our actions.[1] As stated before, every health care provider, both professional and nonprofessional, management and non-management, can be held accountable for acts of negligence. Specific liability will vary on the basis of job descriptions, policies and procedures, and, in some cases, unwritten customary practice. However, every employee does have responsibility for his or her own actions and, therefore, corresponding accountability for those actions. Negligent acts may be overt actions or failures to act (omissions). A housekeeper mopping the floor who fails to place the "wet floor" signs may face liability if someone is injured because of that failure.

In the clinical unit different aspects of patient care may be delegated to a variety of staff categories. However, meeting the basic safety needs of patients is a legal duty shared by all staff. If the side rails are not placed in an upright position for the patient who has been sedated, the person who failed to replace them will be the primary defendant if the patient falls and receives an injury. That staff person may be a nursing assistant bathing the patient, a lab phlebotomist drawing blood from the patient, a respiratory therapist providing a breathing treatment, a student nurse administering a medication, a resident, an attending physician, or someone else.

LEGAL VERSUS ETHICAL ACCOUNTABILITY

Nurses often express concern regarding their responsibilities for various ethical issues, and they should be aware that their legal and ethical responsibilities are not identical. In some areas, the courts have not reviewed a case involving a particular ethical issue. In those areas, then, a legal standard for that issue does not exist. In the absence of a court decision, the nurse must be guided by the ethics of the profession and by personal moral standards. Where the courts have reviewed an ethical issue, some guidelines do exist. However, these guidelines are not comprehensive and do not answer many of the questions posed by the nursing profession. As stated already, the law requires a basic minimum standard, whereas the ethical standards of the health care professional may require a higher standard of care in a particular situation.[2]

The nurse's right to raise objections about patient care issues seems to revolve around ethical issues which society generally has identified as being problematic. If the patient care issue crosses the line into per-ceived criminal conduct or neglect, nurses have been instrumental in bringing those cases into a public forum. However, when the nurse makes an individual, independent decision not to care for a particular patient, the court's review of the situation may not support the nurse's position. For example, if the nurse refuses to care for an AIDS patient because of a value judgment about the patient's life-style, the court will not permit such a refusal. But if a nurse refuses because she is pregnant and fearful of the effects of communicable disease exposure, the court may permit that decision. Generally the court will evaluate whether a rational basis exists for the decision.

Generally, too, the court will consider the public good when deciding an issue. In one case a nurse refused to dialyze a terminally ill patient because of moral and ethical objections. She was terminated from employment and sued for reinstatement. At trial, guidelines from the American Nurses' Association Code of Ethics were presented into evidence.

> The nurse provides services with respect for human dignity and the uniqueness of the client unrestricted by considerations of social or economic status, personal attributes, or the nature of health problems.

The nurse's respect for the worth and dignity of the individual human being applies irrespective of the nature of the health problem. It is reflected in the care given the person who is disabled as well as the normal person, the patient with the long-term illness as well as the one with the acute illness, or the recovering patient as well as the one who is terminally ill or dying.

If personally opposed to the delivery of care in a particular case because of the nature of the health problem or the procedures to be used, the nurse is justified in refusing to participate.

If the nurse must knowingly enter such a case under emergency circumstances or enters unknowingly, the obligation to provide care is observed. The nurse withdraws from this type of situation only when assured that alternative sources of nursing care are available...

This argument was rejected. The court stated that the code of ethics defined a standard of conduct beneficial only to the individual nurse and not to the public at large.[3]

A problematic issue is child abuse, which continues to rise annually and which has become a well-recognized cause of morbidity and mortality among children in the United States. The health care provider's legal and ethical responsibility is to report suspected child abuse victims. Many states require nurses and physicians to report known or suspected cases of abuse, and emergency room personnel should be especially alert to this problem. Failure to detect child abuse may impose liability on the health care provider, including possible criminal prosecution. Nor should the nurse be afraid to report. Most mandatory reporting laws grant immunity from civil suit to those who are requested to report if they have reported in good faith.[4] On the other hand, in many jurisdictions there is no law requiring the reporting of elder abuse; therefore, the decision to assume an affirmative legal duty does not carry an immunity protection. However, the nurse may choose to assume the risk of liability and follow a higher ethical mandate.

In daily practice, nurses experience many different scenarios which have ethical implications. For example, a nurse may give the wrong medication to the patient but the patient does not realize this has occurred. Should the nurse disclose this information to the patient? Must the nurse disclose? From the legal perspective, this evaluation is based on the issue of physical harm or injury. If the patient has been harmed or may be harmed through future effects of the medication, the nurse has a legal duty to disclose. If, however, no physical harm has or will occur, the nurse is not required to disclose.

Applying an ethical analysis to the same circumstances, one might argue that even though physical harm has not occurred, there is harm. Placed in the most negative light, a vulnerable patient without adequate knowledge has been the victim of fraud by a health care provider. Most nurses, faced with this quandary, choose to follow a higher-than-legal standard and to disclose the incident to the patient.

In some situations, the failure to disclose information can be a basis for liability. This is particularly true if proof can be provided that fraud or misrepresentation is the basis for the nondisclosure, and a misrepresentation claim may significantly influence the jury's evaluation. Since misrepresentation may occur in writing as part of the patient's medical record or in an oral conversation with the patient, the misrepresentation in many instances may be the omission of information.[5]

THE GROUP SITUATION

As the health care delivery system increases in complexity, the role of the professional nurse has become increasingly difficult. Compounding this difficulty is the current nursing shortage. Although many factors have contributed to this shortage, including broader job opportunities for women as well as an artificial deflation in nursing salaries over a number of years, nurses have identified actual working conditions as a significant issue. They have pointed to problems related to working weekends and different shifts as well as problems regarding relationships with other health care providers in the clinical units.[6]

These complaints reflect the complexity of health care delivery which mandates a *team approach* to patient care. Despite this, nurses often feel that they are responsible for everything that happens to "their" patient. Even though they view themselves as members of the health care team, and even though they lack control over many aspects of patient care, nurses frequently express this belief and feeling. For example, patients commonly ask nurses for information regarding a diagnosis when physicians have chosen not to disclose it. Obviously, the nurse should communicate the patient's request to the physician, but nurses commonly ask, "Is this enough?" If the physician continues to refuse to disclose significant information, the nurse should contact his or her supervisor and the chain-of-command policy should be followed.

Less commonly, nurses may become involved in unethical situations simply because they are in a team, as is pointed out in previous chapters. In a Philadelphia case, a physician was prosecuted for failing to resuscitate a potentially viable fetus following an abortion. The nurses who followed the physician's order not to resuscitate also could have been prosecuted as accessories to a crime. In another case over two decades ago, parents of an infant born with Down's syndrome refused to allow a minor surgical repair for a congenital atresia. The physician wrote an order not to feed, and the baby slowly starved to death in the newborn nursery. Obviously, the nurses who followed this order were placing themselves in a dangerous situation. Simply because a family and a physician agree upon a certain course of treatment does not make it "right" from the ethical standpoint and, in addition, may be into a violation of criminal law.

Needless to say, what is "right" in the health care delivery system is not always easy to define, and even among themselves nurses may disagree. For the individual staff nurse, communicating with the nurse manager may help to clarify the situation. The nurse manager may have a more experienced perspective and may even have faced the same or a similar ethical dilemma in the past. In this connection, each clinical unit should consider initiating educational programs, particularly with a case study focus, to allow all staff members to verbalize and begin to communicate various ethical perspectives. The ethics committee may also give assistance. Finally, the American Nurses' Association Code of Ethics provides some general guidance to the individual nurse.

As nurses (and other health care providers) move through their educational programs, a professional standard of ethics is developed. The continuation of this development, upon completion of the formal educational program, is the responsibility of the individual as a professional. With changes in technology and reimbursement, the entire health care delivery system is in a state of flux, and ethical issues have become more complex. Although general guidance and assistance may be available to the nurse through these mechanisms, the determination of what is "right" is ultimately an individual decision.

NOTES

1. Fiesta, Janine, (1988). *The law and liability: A guide for nurses* (2nd ed.), New York: Wiley.

2. Ibid., p 213.

3. Warton v. Toms River Community Hospital, 488 A.2d 229 (N.J. 1985).

4. Fiesta, Janine, *The law and liability:A Guide for Nurses*, p. 233.

5. Fiesta, Janine, Nurses' duty to disclose, *Nursing Management, 19* (1), 30—32.

6. Ringold, Evelyn, (1988, August). Nursing in crisis, *McCall's.*

Afterword

In order to avoid legal pitfalls, the nurse should function as a professional, be accountable, and demand respect from others as a person and a professional. Nurses' clear communications to management about concerns with patient care are an important component of health care delivery because nurses are the experts at the bedside. Avoiding assumptions is a part of this duty.

Since nurses are functioning as professionals side by side with physicians, they also need to understand what these respective roles should be. Nurses should make rounds with physicians on a daily basis, not to carry the chart or to take "orders", but rather to learn about the patient's medical condition and to teach the physician about the patient from the nursing perspective. The assumption that the nurse is only present to take orders is erroneous, since, as we have seen, there are times when the nurse is called upon to follow his or her own professional judgment (see Chapter 5).

Recently, litigation has begun to appear dealing with physicians' abuse of nurses. Clearly setting limits for physician behavior is an important contribution that each individual nurse can make, since toleration of incidents of abuse only serves to reinforce such negative behaviors. For striking a nurse during surgery, urologist Jagmohan Desai has been placed on probation for 2 years and fined $2,000 by Nebraska's health department. At a hearing he admitted that he thumped 63-year-old Eileen Belbille on the back when she bent to pick up drapes he had discarded on the floor.[1]

In *Baca v. Velez*[2] a nurse at a hospital in New Mexico worked in the operating room and was in charge of instruments. A disagreement occurred between her and an orthopedic surgeon regarding certain instruments, including an osteotome or bone chisel. During the disagreement, the nurse alleged that the doctor jabbed her in the back with the sharp end of the instrument. The nurse brought an action alleging assault and battery. In order for an assault to occur, there must be an act, threat, or menacing conduct which causes another person to reasonably believe that he or she is in danger of receiving an immediate battery. The jury found that the actions of the defendant did not meet the necessary legal definition.

Respect for one's self and for others as professionals is essential to a well-integrated, smoothly functioning patient care delivery system. Recognition of the individuality of the patient has long been an essential component of the nursing profession, and recognition of the strengths of one's colleagues as professionals can only lead to better patient care.

NOTES

1. (1992, March). *American Journal of Nursing.*
2. Baca v. Velez, 833 P.2d 1195 (N. Mex. 1992).

Index

V

W

Z